YOUR
PANDEMIC
PUPPY

REVODANA PUBLISHING

81 Lafayette Avenue, Sea Cliff, N.Y. 11579

ISBN: 978-1-943824-50-2

www.revodanapublishing.com

YOUR PANDEMIC PUPPY

Finding and Raising
a Well-Adjusted Dog
During COVID-19

Marty Greer DVM JD

REVODANA
PUBLISHING

Your Pandemic Puppy

The first few months of 2020 started off like any other year. And, then, suddenly, the world shut down.

As the news of a novel strain of coronavirus spread, so did the realization that there were inadequate supplies of ventilators, medical supplies and personal protection equipment (PPE) to face the crisis. Health-care workers dressed from head to toe in impermeable suits, and all non-critical medical care, both human and veterinary, was suspended.

For the first time in history, healthy people quarantined in their homes for months on end. With schools closed, parents were thrust into the roles of teachers. Professional educators scrambled to teach online. Employees were told to work from home, setting up offices in basements and on kitchen tables.

With restaurants, bars and most stores closed, our homes became our workplaces, our classrooms, our restaurants, our hospital wards, our hotels, our vacation spots, our hair and nail salons, our world. People stopped venturing out for any but the most essential errands. Carry-out food became the norm, and the world learned to sew pretty face masks.

Enter the one sure-fire way families could keep their sanity – a "pandemic puppy." After the kids had spent months or years begging for a dog, how could Mom say no now? What was Dad's reason to put it off any longer? With all this free time on your hands, why not get that new puppy?

Stuck at home, amid whining kids and spousal spats, having a new puppy as a distraction, a source of joy, something to do, just seemed like the right move.

But at the very time getting a puppy seemed like a great idea, the availability of dogs grew severely limited. Dog breeders, shelters, rescue groups and foster organizations soon found that puppies were "flying off the shelves" as quickly as paper towels and hand sanitizers. Breeders could not supply enough puppies to meet demand. American Kennel Club registration of purebred puppies skyrocketed for the first time in years. Shelters and rescues soon found their kennel runs empty. Foster homes snapped up dogs right and left.

As this book is published, the COVID-19 pandemic continues to be a daily reality for all Americans, and looks like it will be for the conceivable future.

If you are considering getting a puppy or dog, or if you have recently added a canine family member during this topsy-turvy period of your life, this book is a great resource for you and your family. It will help answer your many questions and assist you in working through the bewilderment of understanding what your new canine friend needs to be a happy, healthy, well-adjusted, well-fed and cared-for member of your clan.

This is your great opportunity to select, raise and grow with a new puppy or dog in your life. With fewer avenues to socialize our puppies and new dogs, we now have the time to spend at home to help mold that new arrival into the most perfect pet he can become. Your new canine companion will make you laugh, cry, get out of bed at funny hours, go outside in terrible weather, go on long walks in beautiful weather to places you would not otherwise be motivated to go, and in general help you see the world in a whole new way. She will be someone who will listen when no one else cares, and comfort you when you are alone. He will be an ice breaker for you when you otherwise feel invisible to the people around you, and can become your constant companion.

Although at times you may feel exasperated, frustrated or overwhelmed, your overall quality of life is likely to be greatly improved by adding a furry member to your household.

Becoming a dog owner in the midst of a global pandemic brings with it special challenges. During this time, we have stopped shaking hands and congregating in large groups. Even something as simple as making a veterinary appointment is challenging. Signing up for dog-training classes can be as hard as finding a preschool for your children. Socializing a new puppy during the COVID-19 restrictions has become more difficult; you can no longer just hop out of the car and have your new puppy wander through the pet store with you, picking out new toys and treats. Helping a new dog adjust to seeing strangers in face masks takes extra time and special attention. All of us are left wondering just what dog ownership will look like in the future.

As a result of COVID-19, the relationships that veterinary staff have with their clients have had to change in many parts of the country. Many veterinary clinics are limiting visits, allowing only the pet to enter the hospital via curbside service. As a result, pets no longer have the security of their owner's presence to get them though a veterinary visit. Owners can't watch their pet's exams, unless done via video-conferencing. Veterinary team members have lost the interaction with clients, not being able to read their facial expressions and body language during difficult discussions. In some cases, trust has been lost. In others, curbside service has made the visit less complicated by not having to troop the entire family through the lobby, into the exam room and back to the minivan.

My veterinary team has been serving our rural community for four decades. This level of experience, with literally hundreds of thousands of examinations, diagnoses and client communications, has given me the opportunity to share this information with you, the new puppy owner.

This book is about Pandemic Puppy Ownership 101, and is intended to be short, readable and concise. At a time when we're rethinking almost everything in our lives, *Your Pandemic Puppy* is meant to help recalibrate your concept of puppy rearing and dog ownership.

In these pages, you'll find information on all aspects of your new puppy's physical and mental well-being. From selecting your new companion, through training and medical care, this information is up to date, contemporaneous and thoughtful. (As always, no book, including this one, is a substitute for professional veterinary care.)

But more than just how-to advice, this book also explores what owning a puppy means to a family. It pushes aside some urban legends regarding spaying and neutering, replacing them with new approaches to helping you manage your dog's longevity. It covers the most current parasite-protection products. Included is very important insight on how to help your new dog integrate into your family, both while you are home now and when you return to your former work and school schedule.

This book is intended to help you have a great experience all along the way, from selecting your new puppy through adolescence. Having a new puppy or dog should be lots of fun.

Here's to making that your new normal.

CHAPTER 1

Should You Get a Pandemic Puppy?

The decision to get a new puppy or dog, or to foster a homeless dog, is an emotional one. But it should also be a logical, fact-based decision that you have thought through completely. Jumping into dog ownership should never be a spur-of-the-moment decision. Be certain you and your family have considered all the pros and cons.

Pros

Why should you get a dog instead of a goldfish? At a time when your friends and family may discourage you from adding to your stress level, you may find a new dog or puppy is just what you need.

There are many reasons dog ownership is on the rise, and is rising even faster during the pandemic. These reasons may include some or all of the following:

- Your job is now in your home office. You have the time, space and bandwidth to have a dog under your desk.

- Your work situation hasn't changed much since the pandemic started, and you need someone who is happy to greet you when you arrive home. When there are no after-work activities to look forward to, coming home to an empty house can feel very lonely.

- You have extra time at home, even if you are working or schooling from home. This is a great time to spend raising, socializing and housebreaking a puppy.

- You are under- or unemployed and need someone to talk to and who will listen to you.

- You need an excuse to get out for some exercise. There is no better way to be motivated to go on a walk than to have two big brown eyes pleading with you to get out for some fresh air.

- You need someone to hang out with you at dinner and in the evening while you watch TV, read or work on the computer.

- Your children have been begging you for a puppy since they were able to talk. Now, they are old enough to learn the responsibilities of pet care.

- You may have chosen not to have children and find a dog to be a great addition to make your household feel complete. Nurturing a puppy, having another being with a heartbeat in your home, can make you feel more connected to the world. This is particularly helpful at a time when quarantines and mandates to socially distance leave us all lacking emotional and physical closeness to those we love.

- Your kids have moved out, taking their pets with them, and the house seems too empty.

- When you walk through the door of your home, your spouse/partner might grunt a greeting. But your dog will charge to the door, tail wagging, thrilled to see you. What a great feeling this is!

- You want to vacuum the house more often.

Cons

Just because you have time now, be certain you have considered what happens when you return to work and school, if and when you do. Traditional classrooms and workplaces may have changed temporarily, or permanently, depending on your situation. If you continue to stay at home, the puppy will continue to have companionship. If you are returning to the workplace or going back to school, the puppy will be alone for periods of time – something he was not acclimated to during the COVID-19 pandemic.

- When you go back to your previous schedule, how many hours will your new puppy be alone? Will there be someone who can let the puppy out for elimination and exercise during the day? Will you have time before you leave in the morning to feed and care for the puppy? After work, will you have other obligations such as meetings and kids' activities? When you get home, will you have the time and energy to play with and walk the puppy? Or do you believe you will need time on the couch to decompress? If the puppy has been crated or alone all day, how will she burn up the energy she saved while you were gone?

- If being home with your partner, spouse, children and other family members has been stressful, will a puppy add to the stress? Or will a new puppy give you an outlet to get out for walks, and distract you from other stressors in your life?

- If your income has been reduced by changes in work, will you be able to afford the expenses of a new puppy? There will be veterinary care, including vaccinations, parasite protection, and spaying or neutering. What about the new shoes the puppy chewed up? Can you afford to replace them? What if there is a medical emergency with the dog?

- Keeping the house clean and orderly can be made more difficult with a new puppy or dog. There is extra hair, dribbles around the water bowl, toys left strewn about, and the inevitable puppy accident on the floor. Don't plan on getting help from your partner, spouse or the kids – it will all be up to you.

- Seasonal considerations are also important. While some people detest winter, others find housebreaking a puppy in cold weather to be more efficient: Just like you, your new puppy won't want to spend much time out on a cold, blustery night, and the cold tends to make them proceed with their housebreaking faster. On the other hand, being outside for hours at a time at the more pleasant times of the year has its advantages. Be prepared either way – you will be making frequent trips outside, in daylight and in the dark.

The Final Decision

Some people say, "It is better to ask for forgiveness than permission." This should not hold true when deciding to get a puppy. Your entire household or family needs to be in agreement. Having a new puppy or dog in the home means that increased time spent caring for the puppy will take away from other activities or spending time with family. It means a financial burden. It means changes in where and when you sleep. It may mean asking family to provide care while you are at work, school or traveling. This is likely to be a 15-year commitment.

> Calculate all the pros and cons. Making a list of the advantages and disadvantages in writing can help you make an intelligent, well-thought-out, factual decision.

Whenever it came time to purchase a new car, my ever-practical father frequently said, "Don't love something that doesn't love you back." The great thing about a puppy is that she will love you back. So don't leave out all of the emotion – that takes the fun out of making a decision with your heart.

Take the time and conscious effort to make a well-balanced and well-researched decision. Then relax and enjoy your new puppy.

If you have already acquired a new puppy or dog, have you found that the new puppy isn't all sweetness and light? While we can't have all the answers for you, we can help with the medical and behavioral concerns that your new ownership responsibility has brought along.

Read on!

CHAPTER 2

Where to Get Your Puppy

There are many options for obtaining a new puppy or dog, and there are no right or wrong answers – just opinions. There are purebred and purpose-bred dogs, and there are dogs we can classify as "randomly sourced." The people in each camp may be well entrenched and strongly opinionated, based on their life experiences and life stage.

Because there are so many choices, you need to research, soul-search and discuss choices with your friends and family.

This book is not meant to sway you in any direction, but rather to inform you of the pros and cons of various dog sources. There may be points made here that you had not considered. The most important thing is that you are comfortable with your decision, as you will have years to look forward to spending time with your new bundle of joy.

Rescue Organizations

Many families find obtaining a puppy or dog from a rescue organization appealing. It makes them feel good – they have saved a life. Most rescue groups have a strict application process and will require this pet as well as all others in your home to be spayed or neutered, cats included. During the onset of the pandemic, spaying and neutering services were limited. So limited, in fact, that if you had a cat that was not spayed, some organizations refused to place an already neutered or spayed dog in your home.

In most cases, your rescue puppy will have a start on his vaccinations and dewormings, may already be spayed or neutered, and have paperwork required for transport.

Some rescue groups work only with one breed, while others work in specific regions of the country or world. Research the rescue group before you decide that it is the one for you. Don't allow your desperation to obtain a dog during the pandemic to cloud your judgment about the group you work with or the dog you select. If you miss out on one, there will be another coming along. Believe that everything works out for the best – waiting may allow an even more perfect dog to come your way.

Most rescues require a signed contract with the terms of dog care included. Be certain you understand and can abide by the terms before you commit to the decision. Some rescues will require you to return the dog to them if you do not comply with their terms.

Sometimes dogs come with health problems, such as heartworm disease or allergies. Others have behavioral issues such as fearfulness, anxiety or aggression. Ask about what the dog's triggers are before

14

you decide this is a dog you want to live with. If those triggers are not compatible with your lifestyle, find out before you commit to becoming the new home for this special dog.

Unlike many breeders, most rescues will not replace the puppy if there is a health problem or concern.

Some rescues and similar organizations are importing dogs into the United States legally. However, some disreputable groups are smuggling a disturbing number of dogs across the border, by car or private airplane, without appropriate health certifications and authority. Some of these dogs can carry rabies, screwworms and other exotic diseases that can be zoonotic, or transmissible to humans. While it seems like you are "doing the right thing" by saving such dogs, the health risks for both dogs and humans are enormous.

Legislation is pending to manage importations of these dogs, but literally hundreds of thousands have entered the United States in this manner and will continue to do so without appropriate enforcement of current and future laws. Do not be a party to assisting this, as it may put the health of your other pets and your family at risk.

Another caution: Some "rescue" groups are beginning to breed dogs to create a revenue stream. Sadly, this was not the reason rescue groups were started.

Shelters and Humane Societies

There are many local humane societies and animal shelters scattered across the country. In years past, this was where dogs found as strays or that had been relinquished by their owners ended up.

However, this has changed in the last decade. In the northern tier of 35 or so states, there are no longer enough dogs to meet the needs of the public looking to find a pet dog. (Please realize that cats are a completely different story.) In the southern tier of 15 or so states, there is an overabundance of dogs in shelters and humane societies. This problem is magnified during natural disasters such as hurricanes and forest fires.

Many times, the dogs in the southern shelters or rescues are sent to the northern groups, a process now called "humane relocation." Often, the dog at your local shelter has been caught or relinquished, assessed and transported across many state lines. Next, he has been placed in a local rescue or shelter.

These dogs may have had a tough life, both before they ended up in the shelter or after, during housing with strange dogs, transport, handling, processing and finding a home. It's no wonder some are anxious or fearful.

Most organizations have a process of assessing dogs for behaviors such as aggression at the food dish and how they allow for touching and restraint. If you find yourself drawn to a particular dog, be sure you have the whole story on his behavioral assessment before you make a commitment.

Be very aware that in the current climate of dog rehoming, many shelters and rescues now want to be considered "no kill." While this can be appealing, it has a downside as well. In years past, dogs that showed aggressive tendencies toward people and children were deemed unadoptable and euthanized. While this seems harsh, it was the safest way to handle a dog that could be unpredictable or aggressive.

Now, because of societal pressure and the perceived guilt associated with euthanizing a behaviorally unsound but otherwise healthy dog, many dogs that formerly would have been euthanized are finding their way into the homes of unsuspecting owners. As sad as it is to have to euthanize a dog, human safety should take priority. Be very careful – again, ask to see the assessment of the dog you are considering.

New dogs may not show their true colors, or behavior, until they have been in their new home for about 90 days. Just like an employee with a new job, they are on their best behavior – they come to work early, don't dawdle at lunchtime, and don't smoke in the bathroom. But once they are off probation, they may start to develop into a less-than-ideal employee.

Similarly, when newly adopted dogs become comfortable or at ease in your home, they may start to exhibit undesirable or even dangerous behaviors.

Be on guard for this and immediately consult with an animal behaviorist – not just a "dog trainer." If that professional's assessment confirms that the dog's behaviors make it unsafe for you and your family to continue to live together with him, be prepared to take the action of returning or euthanizing this dog. Don't make excuses for the dog's aggressive behavior. Not all aggressive dogs were abused. Some are just wired wrong genetically. Like people who have committed a violent crime and are a danger to society, these dangerous dogs don't belong in your home or anyone else's. They are just too risky to live with.

In short, don't be tempted to make up reasons the dog is misbehaving to the point of allowing someone to be hurt.

Although this decision can be heart-wrenching, making the right decision to keep your family safe is essential. If the dog is dangerous or aggressive, don't try to rehome the dog. Be honest and be safe. You can't undo an injury or replace a family member, so be prepared to do the safe thing if necessary.

FOSTER CARE

Many rescue organizations, shelters and humane societies use foster homes to help house dogs. For years this is been a successful way to not only reduce the number of dogs in rescue and shelters, but also to assess dogs and help integrate them into homes. By being fostered in a real home, dogs learn how to live as part of a human family, become housebroken, play with toys and other dogs, and develop other life skills that can help find them their forever homes. Of course, sometimes the foster-care home becomes the forever home – what is affectionately referred to among rescuers as a "foster failure."

During the COVID-19 pandemic, shelters have leaned even more heavily on foster homes, leaving shelters nearly empty, and new dogs and puppies harder to find coming through the rescue and humane-relocation system. This is a great thing for the dogs. But it has made it harder for people actively seeking new pets to find new dogs and puppies.

Friends or Relatives

Many people purchase or acquire a dog from someone they know – a friend, relative or co-worker. This can be a great choice when it is someone you trust, and when the parent of the puppy is a dog you already know. This improves the chances you will get a dog you know something about and believe you can live with comfortably.

Breeders

This is the source you can go to for the most information and control over the dog you are going to spend the next 15 years with. Breeders live, eat and sleep with their dogs, quite literally. They know their dogs inside out.

Defining and assigning terms to the different types of breeders is a challenge. No matter how it is worded, classified, defined or named, it is likely someone will disagree with a term is used or be insulted by a term applied to them or someone else. To make it more difficult, some categories overlap.

There are several types of breeders. Most litters from breeders are "purpose bred," meaning the litter was produced from a male and female dog selected by the breeder to be bred on a planned schedule.

A planned breeding usually is from a pair of dogs that were intended to be in a breeding program. Every now and then, however, even reputable breeders slip up and have a litter that wasn't planned (by the breeder, anyway). With an unplanned breeding, the dogs may not have been meant to be bred together at that time. Or they may not have been meant to be bred to each other, but are of a quality that they were in a breeding program. Even the best-laid plans can be overridden by a determined female in heat or a male with a relentless sex drive.

Some purpose-bred dogs are purebred – meaning their parents are recognized as a specific breed of dog by a closed registry, which does not register dogs of different breeds that are bred together. Some purpose-bred dogs are of different breeds; in some circles, these may be called "designer" dogs. Some breeders of these purpose-bred crossbreds will just breed two purebreds together generation after generation. In the past, these may have been called mixed breeds or mutts, particularly if they were a one-time combination. There are some registries that accept dogs of mixed-breed heritage.

With all those caveats, here are some common classifications of those who purpose-breed dogs:

• *Hobby/Dog-Fancy Breeders*

These breeders select dogs to breed for the purpose of competing with them and/or maintaining or improving their selected breed. Most of the time, these are purebred dogs. These breeders typically have only one or two breeds, and while no one goes into any endeavor with the intention of losing money, profit is not their primary motivation for breeding. Many dog fanciers have only one litter a year or maybe one every several years, when they need to replace a dog in their home. Many of these dogs have some type of title from performing in competitive events such as dog shows or hunt tests.

Hobby breeders may be the one source that takes the longest to get a dog from. If they only breed one or two litters a year, you need to get on their waiting list as soon as possible. These breeders have a vested interest in making sure you and your new dog are right for each other. They may try to talk you out of their breed if they feel you are not a good match. They will likely interview you before you are allowed to visit them; during the pandemic, Zoom introductions have become a popular first step. Such breeders probably will have you fill out a questionnaire or application. If you are lucky enough to live nearby, they may visit your home, or you may be allowed to visit theirs. Most reputable breeders only raise one or two breeds or combination of breeds.

- ## *Large-Scale Commercial Breeders*

These breeders raise many litters a year and count on this for part or all of their income. They usually have a large kennel facility meant for raising puppies. They purpose-breed either purebred and/or mixed-breed puppies. They may have several breeds of dogs.

We have all heard about the evils of "puppy mills" – a term for which there is no official definition, but which generally refers to commercial breeders who churn out puppies without regard for their welfare. Many commercial breeders, however, can't be painted with this broad brush. In response to increased scrutiny, some have improved their breeding programs and do health screenings on their breed stock. They have cleaner facilities and do a good job socializing puppies and providing environmental enrichment.

While the long-term relationship with puppy buyers that hobby breeders provide is arguably the gold standard, hobby breeders simply cannot meet the demand for purpose-bred dogs, even when there isn't a pandemic squeezing supply. This void is filled by high-volume commercial breeders, who are the source of puppies for pet stores and puppy shops.

- ## *Small-Scale Commercial Breeders*

These breeders have a few litters a year, which may provide a portion of their income. They typically raise their litters in their homes or small kennels, and market them through the internet and social media.

- ## *Casual Breeders*

These breeders, who occasionally produce a litter of puppies, may breed so their children get to see the "miracle of life." They may want to share their dogs with family and friends. They may use it as a minor source of income. These puppies are usually raised in the breeder's home.

What is most important here is that we understand that despite different opinions, these terms defining breeders are not meant to insult anyone or hurt anyone's feelings. Although breeders may have different breeds, different reasons for breeding, and different opinions on breeding, they are all on the same side. Rather than fighting with one another about their differences, breeders need to watch out for those who want to ban or block their right to breed and raise dogs. As long as the American public is seeking puppies that are purpose-bred, breeders should have the right to select breeding stock as they see fit, and produce healthy puppies.

Brokers and Resellers

Brokers are the businesses some commercial breeders use to market and sell their puppies. Some may be breeders, while others may only serve to help move puppies from breeders to new owners. While some brokers are important links in the dog-supply chain, others can be problematic. Some breeders, such as in Amish and Mennonite communities, need to use brokers or sell to pet stores because cannot have a direct business relationship with buyers. Many brokers and resellers, including pet stores, procure healthy, health-screened puppies that are well socialized and cared for. Be certain you are working with a broker, reseller or breeder who has a great reputation and offers health guarantees. Ask for references and do your research before sending money in any form.

There can be scoundrels in any business. Warning bells should go off if you are asked to pay for a puppy with gift cards, cashier's checks or other suspicious methods. If it seems like there is someone doing dirty business, don't send money.

Be suspicious if the seller or broker wants to meet you at a rest stop on the highway or other location that is not where they raise their dogs. This is another sign you may be dealing with someone who is not going to provide you with the dog you think you are getting.

In short, don't trust someone who seems to be running an underhanded business.

Particularly during the pandemic, you may be vulnerable in your efforts to quickly obtain a new companion. Don't be a victim to an unscrupulous party trying to take your money.

Other Options

There are other places people can find puppies, including websites like www.puppyfinder.com, Craigslist and Facebook, and signs posted at the local grocery store. No matter the source, be careful and research the seller carefully to be certain you don't get taken by an unscrupulous seller.

Many Choices

As you can see, dogs can come from many sources. Take your time to decide what is best for you and your family. Don't jump in. Before you go for a visit, be certain how you will make the best choice for you and the new puppy. Leave your checkbook at home if you have not made a firm commitment before your visit.

It is far better to make a second trip to the seller than to make a hasty decision that may turn out to be a mistake. Be patient and thoughtful to ensure you are making the right choice for you.

CHAPTER 3

Narrowing the Search

During the pandemic, the demand for puppies has skyrocketed. Breeders of all kinds are struggling to meet demand. Puppies that were available at the start of the pandemic were planned for months before this unique time materialized.

Pregnancy in a dog is 63 days long. Add to that the eight or more weeks needed to raise and socialize a puppy, and we are four months from a female coming into heat to the time her pups are available to move into your home. Since female dogs only cycle twice a year, you may have a one-year wait until your special puppy is available.

Be patient. Breeders, rescues, shelters – all are being overwhelmed with inquiries, some serious and some just tire-kicking. Response times for inquiries are taking longer than usual because of this increased volume. You may need to send more than one message before someone gets back to you. Be certain you fill out their questionnaires completely and include photographs of your home if requested. This level of cooperation will improve the chances you are selected to take a puppy home.

Breed Selection

There are two general categories of dogs when deciding on a puppy:

> ## Do you want a purebred/purpose-bred dog or a dog with unknown breed heritage?

Rescuing a dog of unknown heritage is meaningful to many people, as saving a life is important to them. This may mean you will end up with a dog with less predictable traits than if you selected a purpose-bred dog. Getting a dog with big feet does not mean you will have a big dog; conversely, little feet don't guarantee a small dog. Many traits are inherited; not knowing the dog's heritage leads to a less predictable pet. As long as you can manage a dog of any size, coat type, personality and activity level, you will find this a rewarding way to obtain a new dog.

There is more detail about what to look for regarding traits or characteristics in the chart at the end of this chapter.

Be sure to review the health records and origin of the puppy or dog carefully before you commit. This includes assessments for heartworm disease and separation anxiety. Be honest with yourself about your ability to manage health concerns, and the associated expenses. Be certain you are prepared to manage the special needs of a dog with potential behavioral issues such as anxiety or fearfulness. These special dogs need more attention and training, and may have costly medical needs for which you need to be prepared.

Review the written contract the rescue organization will likely ask you to sign. This agreement may have specific criteria that dictate the age at which you spay or neuter, if not already done, and other specifics on how you care for and live with your new dog. Be certain the terms are something you can live with before you jump in and take on the responsibility of a new dog.

During the pandemic, the number of dogs in rescue groups, humane societies and shelters, and on websites and in foster care, has dropped. There are many more families than usual that want to be a temporary or forever home for a new dog. The increased competition may mean a limited number of available dogs that you believe will work as a new member of your household. As hard as it is during this difficult time, do your best to resist taking the first dog that is close to suiting your needs. Be discriminating enough to make a great choice on selection, for your sake as well as the dog's.

The advantage of a purebred or purpose-bred dog is the predictability of the dog's characteristics. This includes size, activity level inside and outdoors, and coat type (does the dog shed, or does the dog need grooming every six to eight weeks?), as well as personality, friendliness versus protective behavior, vigor, emotional stability, ability to learn, biddability and social skills.

Of course, not all dogs of the same breed will have precisely the same traits, but your odds are improved when you know the breed or breeds involved and who the dog's parents are.

Don't feel guilty if you decide to purchase a purpose-bred dog; knowing what you are getting is very important, especially at certain phases of our lives. Whether this is your first dog or your last, there are times when predictability is essential in selecting the right dog so you will be able to be her "forever" home.

Even if you have social pressure to "rescue" a dog, the advantages of a purpose- or purebred dog are numerous. Data from the National Animal Interest Alliance and other sources shows

YOUR OTHER PETS

Before selecting a new dog, consider the pets your family already has. Is your current dog a breed that is collegial, and will he be happy to have a new companion? Is the dog you are considering friendly? Do you have a male or female, spayed or neutered? Do you plan to use a dog you already have in a breeding program with your new dog?

How old are the other dogs in your household? Sometimes a new dog is a great way for a senior dog to stay young and teach the youngster the ways of your world; sometimes, a senior pet is overwhelmed by a rambunctious newcomer. Think carefully about your existing senior dog before you dive into new-pet ownership.

Do you have cats, rabbits, rats, guinea pigs? Chickens, horses, other livestock? Is the breed you are considering likely to look at your other pets as prey? A Greyhound moving into a home full of cats or bunnies might not be the best choice.

that in the U.S., we don't have enough dogs to meet demand. The importance of the predictability of purchasing a purpose-bred dog can't be overstated.

Thankfully, we see much fewer low-quality, high-volume breeders, known as puppy mills. Overall as a society, we have done such a great job of spaying and neutering our dogs that in many parts of the country we don't have shelters overrun with dogs needing homes. (The same does not apply to cats, which are an entirely different population.)

Large-scale and commercial breeders have made significant strides in improving the quality of dogs and the care they receive. Many of these breeders are doing recommended health screenings, as well as having clean, sanitary facilities, environmental enrichment and socialization. While the ideal is purchasing a purpose-bred dog from a small-scale breeder who can provide one-on-one support for the life of your dog, in some cases this option may not work for you. There should be no shame in a breeder making a living raising dogs, and no shame in purchasing a dog from a high-quality breeder.

So, if a purebred or purpose-bred dog meets your needs, purchase one. The amount of money you'll spend is a drop in the bucket compared to the money you will spend on him during his lifetime – for food, veterinary care and other ancillary costs.

Plans for Your Pandemic Puppy

Carefully assess your plans for your dog and your expected lifestyle for the next 15 years before you make a commitment. Take your time in making a decision – on breed, sex, coat type and color, energy level and other characteristics. That cute little puppy with the big brown eyes is a long-term and intense commitment.

For many of us, the pandemic has and will continue to make permanent changes in how we live, work and interact with others. The lifestyle you have developed or has been thrust upon you by COVID-19 may not be the lifestyle you will have in the future. You may need to go back to work in a traditional office instead of your home office. You may have to relocate to a new city. The job you had before may disappear. Or you may be able to continue working from home, allowing for an entirely new world of dog ownership. One dog may not be enough!

If you have specific tasks in mind for your new dog, a purebred or purpose-bred dog may be a better choice. For instance, if you plan to hunt with your dog, a Sporting breed would be a great choice. If you are looking for an agility dog, an obedience dog or a pet dog, nearly any dog can fulfill your needs. But a Border Collie in a small 26th-floor apartment in a large city is not likely to be a good fit. Consider the traits of your potential new dog based on lifestyle before making a commitment.

PANDEMIC PRESSURES

Particularly now, during the pandemic, be very thoughtful about the new puppy or dog you want to acquire. The extra time you have at home allows for bonding, training and sharing experiences. But be certain you and your new companion are able to be separated when or if your work schedule, travel schedule and daily routine otherwise change. Keep in mind that socializing your new puppy with your family, their pets and the rest of the world outside your immediate circle of friends will be more challenging yet critical to the ability of your puppy to integrate into society and your ever-changing lifestyle.

Which of the following do you plan your new dog to become?

- **Companion.** Being a pet is the most noble job for any dog. Remember, no matter your other goals, most people need their dog to be a pet, first and foremost. If you don't want the dog you are purchasing to live in the house, you should rethink your purchase.

  Every pet puppy or dog, if bred deliberately (purpose or purebred), should have parents with breed-specific health clearances performed by a veterinarian prior to breeding.

- **Conformation show** – Yes, these are the "beauty contests" of the dog world. Before you wrinkle up your nose, keep in mind this isn't just about looks. Each recognized dog breed has its own written "standard," which describes the appearance, size and personality of the dog. These criteria were developed many years ago for the purpose of ensuring dogs of a given breed could fulfill the specific purposes and jobs for which they were bred.

To meet these needs, the founders and aficionados of each breed wrote down these criteria. For example, Samoyeds evolved to run through snow. For this reason, they need legs that are longer from the elbow to the ground than from the elbow to the withers, or top of the shoulder. Both Pembroke and Cardigan Corgis were developed to herd cattle by nipping at their heels. Being low and long, they can duck under the hooves of the cow when being kicked at, as well as corner and move quickly enough to keep up with the herd.

In all breeds, specific characteristics detailed in the standard – the outline of the dog, length versus height, length of legs, length of neck and tail, shape of the head, coat color and type, athletic ability, temperament, activity level, territoriality, vocalization and interactions with other dogs, people and other species of animals – all play an important role in the reason for which the breed was developed. Studying the breed standard for the dog you are interested in living with will be helpful both before you select your breed as well as after, as you learn to understand your dog's personality and purpose.

Conformation shows and field trials are the only organized dog competitions in which you must have a purebred dog. In general, the dog will need to come from show or performance parents to have a reasonable chance at success. Be sure you carefully select the parents, breeder and individual dog you plan to compete with.

Although many of these dog events organized by the American Kennel Club, United Kennel Club and others have been suspended, delayed or canceled during the pandemic, they are likely to return in one form or another. Some breed clubs have been experimenting with virtual conformation shows complete with judging and awards. Trick dog titles can be earned online with videos shared with judges, as can beginner titles in Rally, a less formal version of traditional obedience.

Other dog events have limited the number of entries allowed. Some competitions will need different facilities with larger or outdoor spaces. Some

HIM OR HER?

The sex of your puppy is an important decision. Even if you plan to spay (female) or neuter (male) your puppy, there are still secondary sex characteristics that make a difference in the behavior of your puppy.

In part, this decision also depends on the gender of a dog already in your home or one that spends time in your circle of family and friends. In general, alternating genders makes for more manageable relationships. In other words, if you have a female, consider purchasing a male pup, and vice versa.

Many people believe females are smarter and easier to train. In many breeds, males are more affectionate and less independent. Even when neutered, males may still lift their legs to urinate, inside your home and on your landscaping. Wait for the next litter if your preferred-sex puppy isn't available when your name comes up on the breeder's waiting list.

facilities will close. But others that previously did not allow dog events may look to them as a new revenue stream to remain a viable business entity.

- **Agility** – Any breed or combination of breeds can compete in this timed canine obstacle course, which is competitive and fun. Look for a puppy that shows the promise of becoming athletic. If you plan to compete at the highest levels, you will likely have better success with a Border Collie or other breed with a family history of great competitive success.

- **Other performance events** – Farmdog trials, Trick Dog, Flyball, Rally, obedience, FastCAT, dock diving, barn hunt and many other competitive events are becoming increasingly popular. These activities are a

BREEDING

Not all dogs can or should be used for breeding. If you hope to breed your dog, here are a few bits of advice before you get too involved.

- **Remember that "good dogs come from good dogs."** Start with an exceptionally well-bred dog from a breeder who has done breed-club-mandated health screenings. Make sure your agreement with the breeder permits you to use the dog for breeding.

- **Health screenings of parents and other relatives are a must.** Most breed clubs have considered the health disorders that are of most concern to their breed. This may be based on frequency, severity, testing available, genetic predictability or all of the above.

Many of the purebred recommendations are listed on the Canine Health Information, or CHIC, website (www.ofa.org/browse-by-breed). Some purpose-bred non-purebred dogs also have health-screening recommendations.

Before you purchase a dog, whether for breeding, performance or companionship, ask the breeder what testing has been done on the puppy's parents and other close relatives. This will help assure you will be purchasing a puppy with a better chance of fewer genetic health concerns than if you purchase from unscreened parents and relatives.

- **Have a mentor.** This may be the breeder you purchased your puppy from, or it may be someone in a completely different breed who great way to bond with your dog while you both stay active and fit. And it's fun to involve the children in these activities, too! Start training basic obedience and recalls early. And purchase a pair of soccer shoes so you can keep up with your dog!

- **Hunting** – Hunting can be purely recreational or competitive as in field trials and hunt tests. Sporting and Hound breeds include those that are flushing, retrieving or pointing dogs, as well as sight and scent hounds. Knowing how and what you plan to hunt will help narrow the breeds you want to consider. Research the sport and join a local hunt club for assistance. This will speed up your success.

has experience in selecting genetically superior dogs to breed.

- **Do not breed a dog from the shelter, rescue or other random source.** When a randomly sourced dog is bred, you don't know what you will get. You cannot predict the offspring's size, temperament, coat type, activity level or health. There are already plenty of randomly sourced dogs available through rescues and shelters. Just because your neighbors or friends comment they would like a dog just like yours doesn't mean when you have a dozen hungry mouths to feed and lots of puppy messes, they will actually step up and take one.

- **Be sure the female is mature, and that you have enough money to pay for an emergency C-section if she gets into trouble during her delivery.** You'll also need room to raise pups, time to socialize them, a list of people who sincerely want a puppy, and the knowledge to proceed. My book, *Canine Reproduction and Neonatology*, is a must-read before you even start genetic screening. It will escort you chronologically through selecting breeding stock, screening, breeding, whelping, raising the pups, and how to manage the stud dog and dam.

Finding a breeding-prospect dog during the pandemic may require even more research and patience than usual. The demand for dogs during this time means breeders are overwhelmed with requests from highly qualified future dog owners.

ADULTS VS PUPPIES

Many breeders have young adult dogs available for sale. The breeder may have kept the dog to see if he will "turn out" for show or breeding, and later decided that one or more traits developed that make him less than ideal for the purpose they kept him for. These traits often do not make the dog any less perfect to be your new pet. Or the breeder may have kept the dog, male or female, for breeding, and they have arrived at an age or number of litters at which they are no longer going to be bred. Many times, these dogs are healthy and middle aged, as well as crate trained, housebroken and eager to be the apple of your eye.

Adult dogs can come from many sources and end up in rescue. They may have been a stray, found with no collar, microchip or other ID. Rarely, they may have been "dumped" a distance from their home and left to find their own way in the world. They may have been relinquished to find a new home. This can happen when someone loses their job or home, has to move across the country, or develops allergies or other health conditions. It also can happen if the dog has a medical or behavioral issue that the original owner cannot cope with or afford to treat.

Age Considerations

Some people want to start off with a puppy so they can mold it into the dog they envision. It may also be important to you to see your puppy grow.

Most behavioral experts agree that a puppy should stay with the breeder and its mother at least until eight weeks. Puppies who stay with their mother and littermates have a reduced risk of developing into reactive, fearful dogs and are more self-confident as adults. Be patient and don't pressure your breeder or rescue group into sending your puppy home before the time is right.

Taking in an adult dog that has left puppyhood behind has its advantages: The dog is likely housebroken, has some trained skills, has matured and is settled in past adolescence, and has reached full adult height. In other words, you have a better idea of what you are getting – or getting into.

Still other people prefer taking in a senior dog that is unlikely to find a new home due to age or health. These dear dogs often were the beloved companions of older people who passed away or can no longer care for them. They may be slower in their activities, or have some medical or housebreaking issues. But providing a loving, caring and comfortable home for dogs in their golden years can make you feel amazing.

Traits and Characteristics

Many personality and behavioral traits are inherited. Some may also have an epigenetic, or environmentally triggered, basis. Puppies from litters with mothers who had great maternal skills are more likely to be self-confident. Selecting puppies from confident, smart, stable parents and grandparents will improve the odds your new puppy will have similar traits.

Ask your breeder or rescue if they used early neurological stimulation, Super Dog, Puppy Culture or other similar programs, and how they handled the puppies when they were very young.

Characteristic	Considerations
Breed	Research breeds online on the AKC website (www.akc.org). Visit breeders in person or via video chat. Read books that describe breed-specific traits to help you know more about each breed.
Purpose/activities planned	It's time for a family meeting so all of you will have similar expectations for the activities you want to your new family member to participate in. This is a life-changing decision, so be sure you have buy-in from the entire family.
Size (height and weight)	Do you have room in your home? Will you be able to carry him in 10 or more years from now when he is old and can no longer walk into the veterinary clinic?
Age	Skipping the puppy phase can have its benefits, so don't rule this out. But sometimes raising a puppy allows you to mold him into the dog you want him to become.

Friendliness with people	Who is in your household and who visits frequently? Do you live in a busy neighborhood with children who burst through your front door without warning? Or do you live in a more remote area where no one shows up unannounced? Do you want a dog that will alert you or protect you when anyone arrives? Or is it important to have a dog happily greeting visitors?
Good with children	Will children and/or grandchildren be interacting with the new puppy? Do you have kids in the neighborhood? Do you live near a school where there will be children going past your yard several times a day?
Inter-dog dominance	Consider other dogs in your family and life and how a new dog would interact with them. Do your family members have dogs? What are the breeds, sizes, ages and what temperaments do these existing dogs have?
Interaction with cats and other pets	Do you have or do you plan to have cats in the home? Do you have rabbits, guinea pigs, hamsters, ferrets, chickens, livestock (including horses), or other mammalian or avian pets at your home that could become a temptation for your dog to chase or injure?
Social skills	What family members will you expect your dog to live with? How many generations may be in your home? Do you plan to have children? Are your kids planning to stay in your home after high school? Do you anticipate your parents or in-laws may move into your home for long-term care?

Vocalization	Do you live in an apartment with close neighbors or in the country? Some breeds are notoriously noisy, so research and choose carefully.
Emotional stability	Consider the flexibility a dog in your life needs to have to adjust to your schedule and traffic through your home. If you have a crazy lifestyle, choose a breed that can roll with the punches.
Territoriality	Sometimes a protective dog has advantages for someone who lives alone or in a rural or remote area. However, if you have a parade of young people in your home, this may become problematic.
Ability to learn and problem-solve	Do you really want a dog that is smarter than you and your family members? It is true – some dogs are able to outsmart us. Or they may just use the eight hours you are away at work every day to engineer their next naughty plan.
Ability to be trained	Being smart and being trainable are not the same thing. Are you OK with a dog that marches to her own drummer? Or do you want a dog that wants to do everything you ask?
Tendency to be mouthy/ destructive	Some breeds are rarely destructive. However, many breeds, including retrievers, are mouthy and may either be destructive or ingest inappropriate non-edible objects. This means you need to constantly dog-proof your home.

Hair, coat and grooming	Will shedding be an issue? If the dog doesn't shed, are you willing to pay for grooming every six weeks? If she does shed, are you prepared to vacuum frequently? Replace your vacuum cleaner annually? Have a robot-vacuum or a hired cleaning person? Does anyone in the family have allergies?
Activity level, indoor	Some dogs never settle; others are quiet indoors. It can be exhausting to have a dog that is in constant motion. What do you want to do after a long day at work? Be a couch potato or head out with the dog for a long walk or run?
Activity level, outdoor	Some dogs are quiet in the house but very active outdoors. Some dogs prefer to spend most of their time outside. What lifestyle do you have and what are you willing to do to keep a dog happy?
Vigor	Some dogs are just downright sturdy; others are more delicate. Ask yourself if you can live with this. How will you manage the dog in your home?
Health concerns	Every dog has potential health issues. Researching by breed can help you predict health concerns and know what you may expect in the future. But no breed or individual dog can have a guaranteed life expectancy or promise of perfect health.

CHAPTER 4

Integrating Your Pandemic Puppy

Now that it's time to bring home your new addition, special care must be taken for travel and introductions. The motion of a car or plane, new sights, smells, textures, sounds – all are new and overwhelming for little puppy brains to take in.

In only a few short days, your new puppy or dog will know your routine, eat and sleep comfortably, and settle into being your new best buddy.

Take lots of photos – you'll be shocked at how fast your puppy grows. Photos with dog beds and pillows will remind you just how little he was when he arrived at your home.

Pre-Travel Preparation

Many times, your puppy is leaving the only place he has ever known. His momma dog, brother and sister puppies, and other family members are being left behind. After an unfamiliar journey, he will be entering a new environment.

A hand towel, receiving baby blanket or T-shirt, rubbed on the mother and other puppies before leaving the breeder or rescue's location, can bring along scents to soothe the puppy during his first few days in your home.

Consider the use of an Adaptil® Junior Collar, which emits calming pheromones that mimic those of a nursing mother. Ask the breeder or rescue to put the collar on your puppy a few days before he leaves to make travel and the emotional transition easier.

Avoid using Benadryl® as a sedative. It is not an anti-anxiety medication and can confuse the puppy by making him unable to adjust to his new and ever-changing environment.

Traveling in the Car

Have at least one person in addition to the driver travel with the new puppy. The driver can concentrate on navigating, while the others can monitor the puppy for anxiety, car sickness or the need to stop for a potty break.

The puppy needs to be secure and safe in the car. Have the breeder or someone at the source familiarize the puppy with a crate and trips in the car so he is comfortable traveling before you take him home with you.

Your puppy should never ride loose in your car. A crate is essential. Accidents happen in a heartbeat.

Airbags can deploy and injure the puppy. The puppy can cause an accident. The puppy can become a projectile. The puppy can escape from the damaged vehicle. A frightened dog can aggressively keep emergency personnel from helping injured passengers. All of these scenarios have all happened to people I know.

A seat belt is second best to a crate. It secures the puppy but doesn't protect from airbags and other trauma. Similarly, raised puppy seats in which the puppy is secured are not as safe as a crate.

If you must have the dog on the front seat, disengage the airbag before you start driving.

Feeding a gingersnap or two before travel can help the puppy's tummy settle and reduce car sickness. Additionally, dogs are less likely to be carsick if they can't see out the side windows, so, again, using a crate is best, especially as your dog gets older.

Traveling Long Distance

Traveling a long distance may involve car travel with you, an airline trip in the cabin or in cargo, or transport by other means such as commercial carriers who specialize in dog transport.

During the pandemic, air travel is possible although limited. This may be the easiest way to transport a new puppy long distances, and is essential for international travel.

Before the puppy or dog sets off for travel, she needs to be of age, inspected with appropriate health papers and vaccines as well as parasite-control products, and comfortable in the transport setting. Have the breeder or rescue acclimate the puppy or dog to a crate similar to the one in which she will be transported. Use appropriate motion-sickness medications (maropitant) and/or anti-anxiety medications (alprazolam, gabapentin or trazodone, for example). Again, Benadryl® and acepromazine are not anti-anxiety medications and should not be used as such. Have the breeder or rescue practice using the crate and medications if needed to familiarize the puppy with the new setting and to adjust the drugs to the appropriate dose.

Be certain you have allowed enough time to contact government and local veterinary officials to have medical procedures and paperwork completed. Make the appropriate veterinary and governmental appointments. In some cases when transporting a puppy internationally, this can take up to one year. Don't forget to book your puppy on the flight!

Settling In

Coming home with a new puppy is exciting for everyone. But too much excitement is, well, too much.

Have all your supplies purchased in advance. (See the shopping list at the end of this chapter.) Purchasing a new puppy should not be an impulse decision. It isn't like bringing home a new vacuum cleaner.

Find out what kind of food the puppy has been eating and either purchase a small bag or ask for one to come along with the puppy. If driving, take an empty water bottle so you can bring along a small amount of water from the breeder's kennel or home to ease the transition. A diet change along with a switch in water and household is a near guarantee your puppy will develop diarrhea.

If you have other dogs, have them come outside to meet the puppy. Don't allow your current dogs to tower over the new puppy, or he will think he has moved into a terrible new home.

If you have cats or other small mammals, including children, allow the new puppy to see them, and them to see him, but through a gate or glass door. This will give each of them a chance to assess their new housemate without risk of injury to anyone. Do not allow your existing dogs to rush toward the new puppy when he first walks into his new home. And, of course, if you have a dog that you even think might be unreliable or aggressive with a new puppy, consult a behaviorist on how to introduce the two.

The first night home can be the most trying – for both of you. Attempt to arrive during daylight hours, so the puppy can see where he has moved to, and can better see where you want him to go potty outside.

ACCLIMATING TO THE CRATE

The best advice is to teach the puppy to sleep in her new crate the first night you have her home – and future ones as well. As tempting as it is to have the puppy in bed with you, for a variety of reasons it is not the best choice.

Some people like to have the crate in their bedroom; others prefer it to be in a more remote area of the home so they can't hear the puppy if she initially puts up a fuss when placed in her crate for the night.

Be certain the puppy has been out to eliminate and you have spent time exercising her to tire her out before bedtime.

Some puppies nap a lot in the evening. This makes them well rested and harder to get to settle when you are ready for bed.

Putting a towel or blanket over the crate can help soothe the puppy. So can the radio, dog-appropriate music or a white-noise sound machine.

If the puppy needs something to do in his crate, have a food-stuffed toy locked in his crate before bedtime. Some options for filling it include peanut butter or spread (make sure no one in your home is allergic); spray or soft cheese, or cream cheese (don't use if moldy – moldy soft cheeses can cause seizures), and liver sausage.

Don't feed the puppy a full meal too close to bedtime or the puppy will need to go outside to potty during the night.

Once bedtime arrives, quietly settle the puppy into her crate, and plan to spend a little time listening to her fuss while she self-soothes and learns to sleep in her own little den. The first night is usually the hardest, because everything is so new for the puppy. A great rescue, foster or breeder will have taught the puppy to sleep in her own crate before you pick her up. Even so, it's all new at your home. Be patient – she will settle, and on the next night will be better able to rest quietly in her crate. Hearing your puppy snore contentedly will be great music to your ears.

Pre-Puppy Shopping List

During the pandemic, many people are shopping online, with a dizzying array of choices.

For size-dependent items, consider ordering from a local store so you can see the items before you drive away or before they are delivered to your door. Crates, collars and harnesses can be hard to select sight-unseen. Purchasing where you can pick up these supplies also helps support local businesses, which is crucial in these financially precarious times.

For items such as flea and tick and heartworm medications, contact your veterinarian to see if they have an online store, curbside pickup or will ship meds for you. This supports your local veterinary clinic. Most important, it allows your veterinary professionals to be involved in helping you select the right medications for your pet, based on age, size, breed and other specific medical needs that online sources are unaware of. This ensures your pet is on the right medications and that you are not unnecessarily duplicating or overlapping medications your pet does not need and you don't need to pay extra for.

Many times, your veterinary clinic will have rebates on their flea, tick and heartworm products, making them more affordable than if you purchase from an online pharmacy.

As with children, toys don't have to be expensive. A cardboard box might turn out to be the most fun Christmas gift you give a child. However, don't cut corners by allowing your new puppy to chew on old socks or shoes – there is no way for your puppy to distinguish between an old shoe and a new one. You can't get upset with a puppy if you trained her to carry around an old sock, and then find her nibbling on a new one. Expect anything you leave laying within reach (or what turns out to be within reach, even though you thought you put high or far away enough) to become fair game for destruction.

Some supplies are worth spending a little extra money, like a really great crate or a collar that won't pop off when your puppy lunges at the end of his leash. High-quality dog food is expensive, but the priciest is not necessarily the best.

Item	Considerations
Collar (quick-release buckle)	Your puppy will need a collar and ID when leaving your property. Avoid leaving a collar with a tag on your dog when in a fenced yard or crate unsupervised, as the dangling parts can catch and cause injury. A quick-release buckle will make removing the collar faster in case of an emergency.
ID tag	This should have your name and cell-phone number engraved on it. Adding some catchy phrase like "Have your people call my people" or "Call my mom, she's freaking out" will improve the chances someone will actually call to return your puppy to you.
Leash	A soft, six-foot leash, for walks.
Long line	Look for a horse lunge-line or any manageable material so you can retrieve your dog if she wanders or bolts away. This can be 10 to 20 feet long.
Head halter	This is the best tool for walking your dog. Like an ox pulls a plow, your dog will pull you with a collar. A head halter works like a horse halter; you can guide the dog gently by controlling his head. It is not a muzzle and does not keep the dog's mouth closed. Popular brands are Halti and Gentle Leader.
Body harness	These come in many sizes and shapes, usually requiring a trip to the store for a correct fitting.

Crate	You'll need at least one, perhaps more. Crates are an invaluable tool when used properly. They can be fabric, metal, molded plastic or fiberglass. Each has its advantages and disadvantages. If the crate is molded plastic, your dog is better protected but can get too warm. Fabric crates are easiest for dogs to destroy by chewing up the fabric and zippers. Metal crates are cooler but dogs can urinate out the side, pull items in that are within reach, and pull at the bars with their teeth, causing damage. You may need more than one crate so it is appropriately sized as your puppy grows, for different locations and purposes, and one for travel in the car. Some crates have additional features like a door on more than one side, or a door that opens right or left. Some have wheels, making transport while inside the crate easier. Talk to the breeder or rescue to see what size is best for your puppy.
Dog bed (indestructible)	We always feel better if the puppy has a soft, absorbent, warm surface to lie on. Sometimes, this can make the puppy too hot. Be cautious as beds can become chew toys and cause intestinal obstructions. They can also soak up urine, meaning your puppy won't mind soiling his crate and making lots of laundry for you. Make sure the bed is washable and will fit in your washing machine.
Bowls	These should be ceramic, glass or stainless steel. Plastic dishes are not advised as they can be chewed up and absorb fats from food, becoming sources of bacterial infections for your dog.

Poop bags	Any bag can be handy on a walk to pick up your dog's stool. This is a great way to recycle that cache of plastic supermarket bags. Special bags sold on a roll can attach with a hook to your leash.
Pooper scooper	This will keep you from bending when doing yard clean-up. There are many styles; some even have lights for nighttime tidying.
Flashlight	For the inevitable and frequent trips outside in the dark. Keep one hanging by the door that you use most when taking the puppy out.
Food	Dog food should be stored in the bag in which it was sold, as the lining is meant for this purpose. Pouring the contents into a plastic container for storage changes the plastic container and food, and not for the better. If needed for storage, simply lower the package into a storage container so the food remains in contact with the plastic liner of the food bag in which the manufacturer shipped it to you. This will keep the food fresh and free from moisture, as well as critters like bugs and mice, which also love dog food.
Kong® or other stuffable toy	These durable, hollow, dishwasher-safe toys can be stuffed with peanut butter and other delicious distractions.

Muffin tin	Metal, not silicone. Serving food in this will slow fast eaters. (Other techniques include freezing food in yogurt, and putting tennis balls in the food bowl so the dog is forced to slow down while eating around them.)
Chew toys	Bigger and more aggressive chewers need tougher toys. Read the labels and test the toys to assess durability. While a lot of dogs like toys with squeakers, many will aggressively chew the toy, remove and kill the squeaker, then no longer have a use for the very expensive toy.
Fabric water-bottle skins	To use, slide an empty water bottle minus the lid inside, and let the puppy go. Makes lots of great noises.
Dog gates	These keep the puppy out of off-limit areas of your home.
Exercise pen	An underused item that's essentially a puppy playpen. Portable and versatile, it can also be used as a gate in doorways that are too wide for most baby gates.
Pet odor eliminator	Buy one with enzymes to break down odors that attract dogs back to the place on your floor where they had an "on-purpose."
Carpet cleaner	A hand-held carpet scrubber is an essential device unless your puppy is perfect. There are several great ones on the market, making a quick clean-up easy.
Bell to hang at the door	This is a great tool to teach your puppy to ring to ask to go out.

Potty pads	Not recommended as a housebreaking tool for any dog but the tiniest who will almost never step outside.
Flea, tick and heartworm preventives	See Chapter 11.
Nail clipper	There are several good ones, some with replaceable blades.
Dremel or Oster® nail tool	Using a grinding wheel (some are cordless and/or equipped with a light) will allow you to gently shape your dog's nails.
Brush and/or comb	Surprisingly, a simple metal "Greyhound" comb may work best for dogs with thick undercoats. A slicker brush or FURminator® is also a good choice, depending on your dog's coat.
Dog shampoo	Pick what you like the smell of, unless your vet prescribes a medicated shampoo. Be sure to dilute the shampoo according to label directions, usually one part shampoo to seven parts water.
Dental-care products	Toothbrushes, toothpaste and chews all work better than simple water additives. (See Chapter 10 for dental care.)
Snuffle mat	Another way to slow down your puppy's eating, but should not be used without you present, or the fabric could become dinner. These are strips of fleece material tied into a mesh backer to hide dog kibble in. You can find do-it-yourself instructions online.

CHAPTER 5

Housebreaking and Crate Training

How do we start housebreaking? You really can tell your puppy to eliminate and elicit the behavior for fast and reliable trips outside, though of course it will take some training. Though it may seem backward, you start with the desired final behavior of going potty outside, then getting outside, then putting the behavior on cue. Puppies inherently don't know it is bad to go potty in the house; it's your job to teach them.

Housebreaking Step by Step

Step 1 – Urinating and defecating in the great outdoors

- Start by **taking the puppy outside the minute he wakes up in the morning, as soon as you arrive home from being absent,** anytime you let the puppy out of his crate, as soon as the puppy is done eating a meal and, yes, as often as possible in between. (If you can manage every 15 minutes, go for it.) That is a lot of outside time!

- **Use the same door every time you take the puppy out** to relieve herself, so there is less confusion.

- **Have the puppy on a leash and collar** before you need to go out with her.

- **Wear a jacket and boots or whatever clothes you need to be comfortable in** while you are outside – you don't know how long you will be out there.

- **Have non-perishable treats at the door** where the leash, collar, jacket, poop bags and flashlight are waiting for the next trip out. Everything you will need must be at the door. If you run to get something, the puppy won't wait. A flashlight will ensure you can see your puppy's performance – when the puppy is squatting in the dark, it is hard to see if he has urinated, had a stool, neither or both.

- **Have a really good, high-value treat ready** to feed the puppy the very instant he levels out after the squat. Don't distract the puppy in mid-job. But great timing with rewards is essential. If you wait until you get back indoors for the treat, the puppy will think she is being rewarded for coming inside. While that is a valuable behavior to reward, your real goal is to reward elimination outside

- Once the behavior becomes consistent, **start adding in the word you want to use for the elimination act.** Any word will do as long as everyone who takes the puppy outside uses it consistently, and it's a word you don't use in daily conversation, which will confuse the puppy. Use phrases like "Hurry up" or "Better go now," and avoid words commonly used in sentences when chatting with others, like "OK."

By consistently using the same word, you really can teach the pup to "go" on command. This will make your life much easier. If you are working outside of your home and are trying to get out the door to work in the morning, you can use the word to remind the puppy to go potty and stay on schedule.

How many times a day? Every 15 minutes – yes, really! So set a timer, leave your jacket, boots or shoes, leash, collar and yummy non-refrigerated treats at the door. You will be going out a lot!

- If the puppy doesn't perform when you go outside, **crate her when you come back indoors and try again in 15 more minutes.** (Or sooner.) If you don't, you will have an "accident" on your hands.

- When the puppy is loose in your house, you must **keep her in view.** You may find tethering the puppy to your waist will prevent that quick trip the puppy makes out of sight to have another "accident."

- Slowly, you can **increase the amount of time between trips outside.** But increase the time very slowly. Keep setting the timer so you don't get wrapped up in computer work or doing the dishes, and lose track of time.

- **When the puppy has an "accident" (or an "on purpose") on the floor or in his crate, take a newspaper, roll it up, and hit yourself on the head**, saying, "Bad human." It is you who failed the puppy, not the puppy who failed you.

Step 2 – Holding "it" until you get the puppy outside

- **There is only one step here: Watch the puppy like a hawk**, know the behaviors your puppy exhibits when he needs to go out, and when you notice them run to the door like mad with the puppy. Waiting just a second too long will mean accidents. Each puppy has his own behavior signals – it may be sniffing the floor, circling or disappearing into an unoccupied room. Have the whole family sensitized to monitoring the puppy. If you think the puppy is about to potty on the floor, make a loud noise to startle him, pick him up, and make a beeline for the outside.

Many times, keeping the puppy tethered to your belt loop or waist with a long leash or line will keep him from wandering into the other room, usually your dining room or extra bedroom, and using the "indoor toilet." If the puppy begins to try to leave your side or is increasingly active, it is time to hit the great outdoors.

THE PUPPY ROOM

Some families have success keeping the puppy in a small, secure, puppy-proofed room rather than using a crate or X pen (exercise pen). The room should have an impermeable floor surface for easier clean-up – your puppy is unlikely to always wait for you. It should have all electrical outlets blocked with outlet covers to avoid electrocution. Cords should be covered with corrugated cord covers to prevent chewing. The woodwork on the doors, baseboards and cabinets, and sometimes drywall, if present, is likely to be chewed on, so consider this issue before there is damage done by the puppy. If you can accomplish these safety measures, keep this puppy room in mind as you read the rest of the information on crate use.

- ### Step 3 – Teaching the puppy to let you know she needs to go out

This is the hardest step, and one many pups don't master until they are close to four months old. But don't be discouraged. Your puppy will learn to communicate with you, and you will learn the puppy's signals and schedule.

You may find using a bell at the door useful. The bell should be low enough for the puppy to reach, but on the door frame, not the door itself. Each time you take the puppy out, hit the bell, and teach the puppy to ring the bell either with her paw or nose. The advantage to using the bell is it stops the puppy from learning bad habits like barking to ask to go out or scratching your woodwork at the door.

You can use a simple bell on a string or an electronic doggie doorbell that has a remote ringer so you can take it with you when you leave the area where the door is located. These doggie doorbells are available on Amazon, and are marketed as Pebble Smart[R], Mighty Paw and Daytech, among others. Don't forget to order batteries.

Carefully monitor your puppy. If he begins to circle or sniff, quickly invite him to go to the door and go out. Encourage your puppy to alert you, without barking, that he needs to go outside to eliminate. Keep treats coming and a leash available for an immediate trip out.

Do you have to take the puppy outside? Only the tiniest puppies who will never step foot outside should be trained to use a potty pad or litterbox. Most puppies will be confused by being allowed to use a potty pad sometimes and then you being upset if they urinate on your magazines or newspapers on the floor next to your recliner. Pick one training technique, either in or out, and stick to it to prevent confusion.

Why use a crate?

A crate is a safe place for a puppy to be when you can't provide constant attention. It speeds up housebreaking. Most puppies don't want to soil where they sleep and eat, so will try to hold their urine and stool until you can get them outside.

The use of a crate is sometimes seen by people as a negative experience. However, used correctly, it can allow you to sleep soundly, or work with great concentration when you are not fretting and distracted, wondering what your puppy is doing now. In many cases, using a crate means you can keep your puppy or dog safe and continue your active lifestyle.

Dogs have a natural instinct to sleep or relax in their "den." A crate in a quiet area of the home is a perfect place for a puppy or dog to escape for a nap or a good night's sleep. Allow the puppy access to the crate at all times, by leaving the door open so he can slip in to catch a nap.

SUBSTRATE PREFERENCES

Ask your breeder or rescue organization what surface or substrate your puppy is accustomed to using for eliminations. Puppies born late in the year in northern climates may be acclimated only to eliminating on snow or ice. When this melts, your puppy may be confused. If the puppy was litter-trained (yes, this isn't just for cats) or trained on artificial grass or puppy pads, real grass may be confusing for her.

If you know what substrate your puppy was trained to use, replicating this at your home can do two things for you: It can speed up housebreaking, as your puppy will understand what you are asking her to do, and it can help you teach your puppy to use a certain part of the yard. By placing the substrate or surface your puppy prefers in the part of your yard you want her to eliminate in, you can make yard clean-up easier and faster.

How To Use a Crate

Strictly keeping children out of the crate at all times, puppy in or not, will allow your puppy to recognize this is her "safe place" to hang out when there is just too much stimulation or interaction.

Crates keep the puppy safe from injuring herself. They keep your possessions safe from the puppy, who don't know what is hers and what is yours. Puppies can get into medications, food, backpacks and trash baskets, and chew up furniture, cell phones, electric cords and remote controls. Chewing up rugs and pantyhose can cause bowel obstructions, necessitating surgery or causing you to lose your puppy without intervention. Medications, cigarettes, and sugarless gum and candy containing xylitol can be toxic to your puppy. Remote controls and cell phones are expensive to replace. Electric cords can cause fatal shocks.

Even when you are working or schooling from home, puppies can quietly slip away and get into trouble. Be very careful, and monitor or crate your puppy to be safe.

Crates can be used as a safe "time out" place for puppies when they need to settle after being overstimulated. Just like children sometimes need a quiet place to decompress when they get over the top, puppies benefit from a short three- to five-minute rest in their crate. No, the puppy won't learn to hate his crate any more than you learned to hate your bedroom when sent there by your frustrated parent. When the puppy comes back out, you will find you are more patient, and the puppy more manageable and ready to learn.

Puppies should not spend all their time in a crate. But you need to have the puppy crated or tethered to your belt so he doesn't slip off unnoticed and have an accident or get into other kinds of trouble. Statistically, an extra bedroom and dining room are the most likely rooms for your puppy or dog to use as his "indoor bathroom." These are the rooms you are likely to catch the puppy sneaking into in the brief moment you take your eyes off him.

The crate can be set up in a bedroom or quiet area off the main living area. Sometimes having two crates makes sense – one in the bedroom for nighttime use and one in more heavily used areas so the puppy isn't "stored" out of sight and out of mind when you are otherwise busy with cooking, the kids or work. You may find it works well to have different styles of crates for different purposes.

KING KONG

There are many toys designed to be stuffed with food to keep dogs occupied, but Kong® was the first to market. It started as a red, snowman-shaped, hollow, firm toy that bounced erratically because of its shape. The Kong® quickly became the darling of the dog-training world when its potential to be stuffed came to light. The toys now come in other colors (black is made of the hardest rubber – handy for the aggressive chewer) and shapes, and other stuffable hard-plastic toys have also entered the marketplace.

When stuffed, these toys are a great way to occupy the puppy's time and attention when you are busy with work, or gone and the puppy is crated.

You can stuff them with anything that fits through the hole that is safe to eat. There are specially marketed aerosol cheese and peanut-spread products, but you can also use regular peanut butter, cream or spray cheese, yogurt (freeze after spooning into the toy), liver sausage, and on and on.

Using the dispenser or your finger, smear the soft food onto the inside to line the entire interior of the toy. Then add your puppy's regular food. Finally, block the exit with a linear food treat like a dog biscuit or hot dog by flexing the toy – this allows an object longer than the round opening to block the exit, keeping your puppy busy longer.

Prior to you leaving or using the toy, stuff it while your puppy watches, so he will begin to anticipate the toy becoming his. Then, put it well out of reach or lock it in his crate, with him on the outside. By doing this, you will help your puppy look forward to being placed in his crate, as he has a busy schedule of emptying his toy ahead of him. You will feel better leaving him for shopping trips or going to work when he is looking forward to getting to his toy. At the end of the session, the toy can be run through the dishwasher for the next time you need it. It is helpful to have several available for this application, including a prepared one ready in the freezer to slow down aggressive emptiers.

When choosing a toy, regardless of brand, be certain it is big and hard enough so the puppy can't chew it up and small enough so his lower jaw won't get wedged in it during your absence.

DAYTIME CRATE USE

During the day, when you are unable to supervise the puppy, a crate will keep the puppy and your personal belongings and floor safe. This should be used for short periods of time. Make arrangements for the puppy to get out for a short midday walk to help with housebreaking. If you are gone for work, find a neighbor or friend who can take your puppy out and have a short play session. The website www.care.com is a great resource for puppy caretakers.

NIGHTTIME CRATE USE

After about three months of age, most puppies can sleep through the night, if you limit food and water access in the last two hours before bedtime. If you have a quiet puppy, having the crate in your bedroom or that of a family member works very well. If the puppy is still acclimating to the crate, you may need to put the crate somewhere more remote so the puppy can learn to sleep through the night. Draping the crate with a blanket can help the puppy rest better. Just be careful the puppy does not start pulling the blanket into the crate and chewing it up, as this can be dangerous.

Having a TV, radio, sound machine or dog-friendly music playing at low volume can help drown out sounds that would otherwise upset the puppy. Putting the crate in the garage or basement where it is too isolated, cold, dark or scary is not a good way to teach your puppy to love her crate.

As with a young child, you may need to be a little tough, leaving the puppy in the crate while she learns to self-soothe. Putting a food-stuffed toy in the crate can help. Of course, be sure the puppy doesn't need to go outside to relieve herself or has a medical need before you pull the pillow over your head and ignore your newest family member.

A soft, absorbent, washable, chew-proof bed in the crate will make it more comfortable for your puppy or dog and help you feel more like you have made a little bedroom for her.

Do your very best to avoid bringing the puppy into your bed at night. It may seem cute at first, but this may lead to midnight trips to the laundromat or bad habits of puppy dominance you will later regret.

Crate-Training Setbacks

Sometimes, no matter how hard you try or how cooperative your puppy is, there can be setbacks. Two of the most common and frustrating ones are when your puppy has diarrhea and when your puppy has a bladder infection.

Diarrhea is very, very common in young dogs. Common is not the same thing as normal – a puppy should normally have a formed stool, firm enough to pick up, hopefully while you're using a glove or bag. However, the intestinal tract is the largest immune organ in the body of any mammal, with trillions of bacteria. Add to that the tendency of all puppies to pick up and swallow everything they can get their furry little lips on, and you have a recipe for disaster.

> When is too much diarrhea too much, and when do you need veterinary intervention?

In general, if the puppy is sick – meaning lethargic, vomiting, not eating – you need care. Or if the diarrhea is unmanageable or persistent, you need care. Avoid home remedies using human medications, as not everything that is safe for you is safe for your puppy. Also avoid diet changes as a treatment, as you may make the situation worse.

Call your veterinary clinic. They will almost assuredly ask you to bring a stool sample in for testing. They may be able to prescribe something to help if they have recently seen the puppy. They may suggest a prescription or highly digestible diet. If the puppy is vomiting, dehydrated and sick, you need to seek an appointment; go to an emergency clinic if your regular veterinarian cannot accommodate the puppy for care.

Bladder infections are less common, particularly in male puppies. It is common and normal for young puppies, male and female, to have a mucousy, sticky discharge from the prepuce (where the penis is stored) or vulva/vagina. This is not an infection – it is normal before puberty. And remember, it is common for puppies to urinate frequently, as often as every 10 minutes. However, if you notice a setback in housebreaking or crate training, increased frequency, or if there is bloody urine, straining or no urine being produced, you likely have a puppy with a bladder infection. If this is the case, contact your veterinarian for an appointment.

Acclimating to the Crate

- **Start slowly**, rewarding time in the crate. Slowly means waiting for your puppy to wander into his crate for a reward in the crate. After a few trips in on his own, close the crate door for literally a second. Very, very slowly increase the time the crate door is closed. The first few increments need to be very short, as rushing will lead to a setback. So, go from one second to two seconds to four seconds, and on and on. Once you get to 30 minutes, you can take a bigger jump to one hour.

- **Feed your puppy in her crate, not the kitchen.** In this way, the puppy associates her crate with a positive experience. It also keeps kids or other dogs from interfering with mealtime.

- **Then teach the command.** Once the puppy is comfortable going into his crate, start using the word you want him to respond to. "Kennel" or "crate" are commonly used terms.

CHAPTER 6

Socialization and Training

Everyone wants a puppy that is smart, self-assured, confident and can adjust to changes as they are dished out. Without great genetics, socialization and being neutered or spayed at an appropriate time, your puppy has a greater risk of becoming timid, fearful, anxious, even aggressive. Helping a puppy to become "bomb proof" is a big task. It starts with your puppy's breeder or other source, and continues with you through your puppy's adolescence.

Training young puppies takes time, but it is time well spent. It is easier to prevent bad behaviors than to unteach them. While you are home more, under quarantine or working from home, take many short opportunities throughout your day to teach skills to the puppy. Short training sessions are more impactful than one long, intense one. All day long, your puppy is learning. Be sure what she learns is what you intend to teach. Make it fun, and use lots and lots of veterinary-approved treats.

During the pandemic, tools and techniques to socialize your puppy have become more restrictive. But with some creativity, you can still raise a well-rounded, well-adjusted puppy.

Words Matter

Dogs don't come with a built-in vocabulary. Just like children, they need to learn a language, any language. Saying the word you want the puppy to learn over and over, louder each time, does not constitute teaching.

When you teach a word, you first catch the puppy performing the behavior, then use the word and immediately provide the reward – i.e., the treat.

Be certain everyone in your puppy's life uses the same word for the same command. Puppies can't interpret synonyms. Words like "come" and "get over here" don't mean the same thing to a puppy.

A pet peeve of many dog trainers is using a command over and over. With kindness in your voice and heart, use the command once and expect the behavior. If your puppy does not respond, either the environment is too distracting for effective training or the puppy does not understand the command.

Additionally, puppies are very specific about the context in which they learn. If you taught your puppy to sit while she is beside you on a leash and she was reliable, and then you ask her to sit when she is off leash and across the room, expect failure. It takes time to learn to do any command consistently in different settings or contexts. Just knowing this will help you understand how your puppy thinks and learns.

When selecting commands for you and your family to use, be certain you don't use a word that will be part of everyday conversation. Words like "OK" to release a dog from a sit will confuse the dog when you use that same word while casually conversing with someone.

You want to be sure you know what behavior you want with each word. When you say, "Sit down," do you want the puppy to "sit" or "lie down"? In my house, "down" means "lie down," but "off" means "stop jumping up." So use whatever words you want, but make sure the puppy gets consistent messaging.

Don't use a word for a command you cannot enforce. You pretty much know that when the puppy is off leash chasing the neighbor's cat, and you call "come," the puppy will continue to chase the neighbor's cat. You now have unfortunately just taught the puppy that "come" means nothing, or, worse, "come" means continue running after the cat. Ensure training is done in a controlled environment in which you can teach the puppy what you want him to learn.

But this does not mean you train for 30 minutes in a classroom setting once a day.

Training happens every day, everywhere. It can be in the kitchen, as your puppy waits when you cut up veggies for dinner. It can be next to the couch while you watch TV. It can be during bath time with your kids. Or under your work desk while you are on a call. Training happens anytime the puppy has an experience she learns from – whether she learns the skill you wanted her to learn or the skill you never meant for her to assimilate.

I once taught my dog to be afraid of homemade liver brownies in just 30 seconds. I was training my first Pembroke Welsh Corgi for the obedience ring. She was sitting on my driveway on a long line, facing me, with her back to our country highway. I was teaching her a long down/stay, using a liver brownie as a training treat. As she was on the long down, a very noisy tractor chugged over the hill. I saw it approaching and assumed she had heard these sounds before and was desensitized to the backfiring and rattling.

Boy, was I wrong. She broke the long down/stay, and made a beeline for the house. (Good thing she was on a long line, or she might have bolted into the tractor's path.) It took me three months to get her to look at a liver brownie again – she associated this once highly prized, delicious treat with the scary noise of a tractor she didn't see coming.

Be careful what you wish for, as your puppy can quickly make a wrong and unfortunate association, even when not in a training session.

A Word About Treats

Use them!

Many people (especially men?) think puppies or dogs should "perform" for them just because they were asked to follow a command. How many of you would go to work the Monday following a missed paycheck on Friday? Not many, I'd say – at least not for more than one shift.

We are asking the same from our puppies. Going outside in the middle of the night in a rainstorm or blizzard to eliminate is asking too much. Puppies know there is an "indoor bathroom" if they can just wait long

LURES, REWARDS AND BRIBES

It's important to understand the difference between lures, rewards and bribes.

In a nutshell, bribes don't work, but rewards and lures, especially in combination, are useful tools in shaping behaviors we want our dogs to learn.

A *lure* is a treat you show the puppy to entice him to do the desired action. An example is slowly moving a treat back and over the dog's nose to guide him into a sitting position. (It is *not* forcing the puppy's bottom to the ground.)

Luring helps the puppy understand the specific motion you are requesting by helping him perform and then reinforcing the behavior. In short order, the puppy will perform the behavior faster and faster with reinforcement.

A *reward* is given to the puppy after the behavior you are trying to teach has been performed. This reinforcement helps teach the puppy what you are asking him to do.

A *bribe* is a treat promised before the behavior when trying to convince the puppy to show a particular behavior. This fails because you have provided the treat before the desired behavior.

Combining lures with rewards shortens training time. Changing up the reward item, such as different food treats alternated with a variety of toys, will keep your puppy engaged.

enough to get back inside. We've all been there – we stand out in the driving rain waiting for our puppy to perform, finally can't take it anymore and as soon as we go back inside, we find a puddle.

The rules for treats are:

• **Make them reaaalllllyyyy good – high value.** Use cheese, microwaved hot dogs, liver or other very delicious goodies to get the puppy's attention.

• **Have exquisite timing when you give a treat**, so the puppy makes the connection between the task and the reward. This means making sure you give the treat in immediate proximity to the performance of the desired action, so the puppy can make the link.

• **Treats are more reliable than verbal rewards.** They are fast, and you can't use them the wrong way. Verbal rewards – how and when you use your voice – can confuse the puppy. Men in particular struggle with the right tone of voice when reinforcing puppy behavior. Sorry, guys, I don't mean to sound harsh, but your body carriage and tone of voice can make training more difficult.

Slowly, treats and toys will be phased out, using the hand-signal lure as a substitute for the food treat.

Training Classes

There are many effective trainers. What is important is finding a trainer who suits the needs of you and your puppy. Before you go, find out what tools and types of training they recommend. If they plan to train without treats or with methods you consider to be "heavy handed," find a different trainer. If you get into a class that isn't right, sacrifice the fee and don't return – this is better for your puppy than creating a phobia from the wrong style of training for your needs.

In-person classes have the advantage of puppy socialization, feedback from the instructor, and peer pressure to practice between classes. During the pandemic and the recovery from COVID-19, online classes or reading the material in a book are better than not training your puppy at all. You may even be able to find online classes on Zoom or another virtual-classroom platform. This allows you to take a class with a trainer who is not local to you.

A word about clicker training: Clicker training – which uses a consistent, short "click" from a hand-held clicker to mark desired behaviors – works very well for some dogs and trainers. Clickers are not remote controls – you don't click to make a dog do something; instead, you click when the dog does or offers a behavior that you want to reward and see more of in the future.

That said, clicker training might not be for everyone. Some dogs are very sound sensitive, especially those with upright ears. Having a dog make an association between the click and the behavior you are trying to capture requires exquisite timing – otherwise, your dog will think she is being rewarded for something entirely different. If you leave your clicker somewhere else when your dog offers a behavior you want to reward, you may need to make clicking noises with your tongue instead, which may not be as precise.

Search YouTube for clicker-training videos and demonstrations to see if this is the right training method for you.

Socializing Your Puppy

To have a puppy that is confident in as many settings as possible, intense socialization is needed while the puppy is still young. The experiences must include meeting a variety of people, other animals, and as many experiences as you can provide: The rule "100 experiences in 100 days" starts from the time your puppy is weaned.

You'll need to work hard to continue providing a wide array of exposures to whatever you can dream up that is safe for you and your puppy.

The difficult part of socialization is balancing the risk of disease exposure and the well-being of your puppy with visiting as many places as possible. The biggest concern with exposure is protecting your puppy from contracting parvovirus, one of the viruses for which puppies are vaccinated. That said, most veterinarians and behaviorists would agree that careful socialization (until 18 weeks, when the puppy develops full immunity) is as essential as protecting against contagious diseases.

Play dates can be a great way to socialize pups. Even during the pandemic, you can find puppies and dogs in need of socialization with nearby owners who are willing to join you: After all, it's only the humans, not the dogs, who need to be socially distanced. Find a puppy or young dog that is about the same size and personality as yours. You don't want either dog to be too dominant or too shy. Be sure to supervise the play sessions for the safety of all involved. Avoid having items of too great a value, or a fight may ensue. Keep the sessions short enough that the pups leave wanting more time together. Consider having both on a long leash or line to allow you to reel them back away from each other should they have too much fun.

DOG-PARK CAUTIONS

Dog parks have risks associated with them, as they are usually unsupervised. This means dogs who are not screened for being compatible may be in the same enclosure at the same time, leading to injuries and scary outcomes. Going to the same dog park on the same days at the same times improves the odds your dog will interact with the same dogs, making it safer. But dog parks also increase the risk of parasite exposure, so be certain to use appropriate flea, tick and intestinal parasite control products. Dog facilities with swimming pools are another great way to get doggie exercise without canine collisions.

During the pandemic and our recovery from it, we may need to be creative in methods of socialization. While you can take an online puppy class to learn training techniques, dogs can't socialize virtually. Your puppy will need real-life exposure to other dogs, animals and people to achieve real socialization. Find creative solutions for methods you can use to improve their social skills and 100 learning experiences.

Socializing and exposure to 100 experiences includes meeting small children and older people, men and women, men with facial hair and women in hats. It includes old and young dogs, small and large dogs, dogs with and without tails, black dogs and white dogs, furry dogs and short-coated dogs.

Before COVID-19, visits to nursing homes and libraries provided great opportunities for socialization. But these types of visits may never again be an option. Pet stores and some hardware stores allow dogs. Doggie day care improves a dog's social interactions with the supervision of professionals while keeping the dogs safe. Keep your puppy's environment interesting and different. Rotate his toys. Give him new experiences. It is OK to give him a chance to get a little frustrated, as he will learn to work through problems. Take care to avoid physical injuries and overwhelming him, or he might become afraid of the challenge. Be careful of temperature extremes – even a warm day can create hot asphalt that can burn the puppy's delicate feet.

Even if your puppy was exposed to an "adventure box" – a stimulating framework with dangling objects that make a lot of noise – she can still benefit from one that you can build or purchase yourself. Avidog (www.aviddog.com) offers a set of plans. Puppy agility equipment, like a mini-dog walk or mini-teeter, is built low to the ground and can be fun for puppies to start learning balance. It's important for your puppy to experience varied sounds, feels and surfaces.

One of the simplest ways you can introduce puppies to varied surfaces – the feel of different textures under their feet – is to purchase a variety of bathmats from your local or online superstore. There are bathmats that are smooth, bumpy, hard, soft, shiny, dark, light, rough and grass-like. Costing under $10 each, they can be swapped out and washed after use. By providing varied surfaces, you can teach your puppy to accept changes.

During the pandemic, coming up with varied experiences can be a challenge. These include exposure not only to a variety of people and dogs, but other normal household and neighborhood experiences. A simple walk down the street can become an adventure. If you venture out on garbage-pickup day, you can help your puppy orient to many sounds, sights and smells: the beeping of a garbage truck backing up, banging garbage cans, the smell of the neighbor's garbage, the sight of a big truck and the view of a neighbor racing to the curb with a last-minute recycling deposit.

Give your puppy choices, and allow him to work through new experiences, without rescuing him. Try to avoid being a "helicopter" owner – keep him safe, but allow your puppy to solve and learn. A puppy who is thoughtful about new challenges is normal – don't misinterpret this caution as fear. Give the puppy time to observe the situation he is wary of. Don't rescue the puppy by scooping him up and cuddling him when he is safely working through a situation. Your reaction has the potential to reinforce a fearful response. Assure yourself your puppy is safe, and gently allow him time to work through a new experience.

Checklist for Socialization

This checklist by Dr. Sophia Yin is reprinted with permission from Cattledog Publishing and www.drsophiayin.com.

The goal is that the puppy has positive experiences, not neutral or bad ones. It's important to watch the puppy's response and note what it is and to also give treats to help ensure the exposure is a success. Here's a checklist that can help you. Download a copy of this puppy socialization checklist at www.drsophiayin.com.

You can grade the response if you want or just check off each exposure.

Progress	Score	Response to the person, object, environment or handling
Needs Work	**1**	**Overarousal or try to get at:** Growl, nip, bark, struggle (for handling) or lunge
	2	**Avoid:** Struggle, hide, try to get away, won't approach, or hesitant to approach
	3	**Freeze:** Holds still (but not eating), non-exploratory, moving slowly or acting sleepy when they shouldn't be tired
Going well	**4**	**Calm, relaxed,** explores the object or environment, playful, **focused on the food**
	5	Calm, relaxed, explores the object or environment, playful, **even without food**

Additionally, a plus sign (+) can be used to denote better progress, and a minus sign (–) denotes not as good: For example, 2+, 2 and 2- are three levels of response.

Week Start Date _____

CLASS OF SOCIALIZATION	SPECIFIC SOCIALIZATION	DAY & SCORE (or check mark)						
		M	T	W	Th	F	S	Sun
Handling	Checking the ears							
	Examining mouth and gums							
	Opening the eyelids							
	Squeezing the feet							
	Handling and trimming the toenails							
	Pinching skin							
	Poking the skin with a capped pen							
	Touching and squeezing the nose							
	Poking the nose with a capped pen							
	Cradling puppy in your arms on its back							
	Holding him in your lap							
	Holding puppy upside down							
	Holding puppy on its back while giving a belly rub							
	Hugging your puppy							
	Pulling the collar (gotcha)							
	Grabbing puppy by other part of body							
	Wiping body with a towel							
	Putting on a head halter							
	Putting on a harness							

Week Start Date _____

CLASS OF SOCIALIZATION	SPECIFIC SOCIALIZATION	DAY & SCORE (or check mark)						
		M	T	W	Th	F	S	Sun
Unfamiliar People	Women							
	People of many ethnicities							
	Tall men							
	Men with deep voices							
	Men with beards							
	Elderly							
	People wearing hats, helmets							
	People wearing Ugg® boots							
	People wearing hoodies							
	People wearing backpacks							
	People wearing sunglasses							
	People with canes, walking sticks or walkers							
	Teenagers							
	Children standing as well as playing							
	Toddlers (walking and squealing)							
	Infants (crawling)							
	People running by							
	Indigent or homeless people							
Unfamiliar Dogs	Dogs who play well							
	A dog who will reprimand puppies with appropriate force and restraint for getting into his personal space							
	With puppies who play well and do not get overly aroused							

Week Start Date _____

CLASS OF SOCIALIZATION	SPECIFIC SOCIALIZATION	DAY & SCORE (or check mark)						
		M	T	W	Th	F	S	Sun
Other animal species	Cats							
	Horses and livestock							
	Any types of pets you may have							
New surfaces	Metal surfaces - such as manhole covers, vet hospital scales							
	Concrete							
	Slippery floors such as hardwood, linoleum or marble							
	Wobbly surfaces such as BOSU® ball, a board on top of a book or unbalanced thick tree branch, a wobble board							
	Stairs							
	Wet grass							
	Mud							
	Ice, frost or snow if you will live in such areas							
Scary sounds	Thunder (CD)							
	Fireworks (CD)							
	Babies and kids (CD)							
	Alarms (CD)							
	Dogs barking (CD)							
	Doorbell ringing (CD)							
	Traffic (like downtown in a city)							
	Jack hammers (CD)							
	Vacuum cleaner (CD)							
	Sirens (CD)							

Week Start Date _____

CLASS OF SOCIALIZATION	SPECIFIC SOCIALIZATION	DAY & SCORE (or check mark)						
		M	T	W	Th	F	S	Sun
Objects with wheels	Skateboards							
	Rollerblades							
	Garbage cans outside							
	Shopping carts							
	Baby strollers							
	Wheel chairs							
	Bikes							
	Cars							
	Buses							
	Motorcycles							
Man-made objects	Pots and pans							
	Blankets or rugs being shaken							
	Brooms							
	Balloons							
	Umbrellas							
	Bags blowing in the wind							
	Sidewalk signs							
	Garbage cans in the house							
	Garbage cans outside							
	Plastic bags blowing the wind							
	Large plastic garbage bags							
	Metal pans or other metal surfaces							
	Metal pens							

Week Start Date _____

CLASS OF SOCIALIZATION	SPECIFIC SOCIALIZATION	DAY & SCORE (or check mark)						
		M	T	W	Th	F	S	Sun
New environments	Suburban neighborhood							
	Residential city streets							
	High-traffic city street (such as downtown)							
	Shopping-mall parking lot							
	Inside buildings							
	Dog-friendly event such as an agility or obedience							
	Location of several different dog training classes							

CHAPTER 7

Life Skills

Maybe they were right – you have bitten off more than you can chew. Your friends and family are going to say, "I told you so." Then there's the little voice in your head that says taking on raising a puppy during the pandemic is too much for you.

But, no, they are wrong. You *can* do it! With the ideas and tips that follow, you will be able to raise a polite, social, well-trained dog that is really fun to live with.

While there is no substitute for a great puppy-socialization class you take in person, with the right tools you can manage your new charge. Look for online classes if you can't take them face to face. Be creative in the ways you socialize your puppy. During nice weather, you can bring a chair and sit outside with your puppy on leash in an area where there are people going into any thriving business or open school. Have a safe snack with you – something that you can hand to people passing by to feed your puppy. Avoid snacks that contain potential allergens like peanut butter.

Keep in mind that small children may not understand the treat you hand them is for the puppy, not for them. By asking people passing you to stop and interact with your puppy, you can create great social experiences, allowing your puppy to learn that people come in many sizes, shapes and appearances. You will want to do this as often as possible, helping your puppy become accustomed to rides in the car, to different destinations, with as many experiences as possible.

Here are some essential life skills to teach your growing puppy, especially as he moves into adolescence:

Wait at the Door

This is often counterintuitive to what we usually let our dogs do. Many of us tend to hold the door open and shoo our dogs outside or inside. This is almost essential when you have multiple dogs in the household. However, the problem is you allow the dogs to have too high "status" when this happens. Too much status leads to pushy dogs. Instead, you need to step through the doorway, have the dogs wait, then allow them through the doorway one at a time.

Door/doorway access is highly valued to dogs. Anything else of high value, like a newly cooked hambone with meat still on the bone, is likely to cause fighting in your household if you have more than one dog. Allowing multiple dogs to charge the door, going in or out, is likely to cause a scuffle. Teach control here.

Preventing Jumping Up

As cute as it is when puppies are little, this loses its charm when your little puppy is a 150-pound oaf and your frail grandmother comes to visit.

Unfortunately, most of us have been taught to "knee" our dogs to stop them from jumping up. Problem with this is, dogs read our body language better than we do. When we lift our foot to knee the dog, we move our center of gravity and shoulders back, which in dog language is an invitation to jump up more.

The better way is to lean into the dog, so your center of gravity – your shoulders – move forward. That body language says, "Don't jump up." Stepping on the leash when the dog is trying to jump on you to keep the dog close to the floor can work, too. When you step on the leash, the dog can't get her feet high off the ground. While this frustrates the dog, it also teaches her that you don't want her jumping.

Like any training method, this works well over time. But if Grandma is coming over soon, keep the dog on a short leash and under control. Going to the ER with a broken hip is no one's idea of having your new puppy make a good impression.

TEACHING YOUR PUPPY A SCHEDULE

During the topsy-turvy time of the pandemic, your puppy won't need to learn your schedule. If you are working from home, you can adapt your schedule to your puppy's needs. When the puppy needs to go out to eliminate, you are there for her. When she is hungry, you are there to feed her. But once or if your life returns to "normal," you may need to return to school or a traditional work schedule, at for least a few days a week.

To prepare your puppy for this transition, attempt to establish a schedule that works for you both. This includes the time you get up and take him outside first thing in the morning, mealtimes, play times, times for walks, and time to go to bed.

Using a crate for some of these skills is invaluable. Having hollow-centered toys pre-stuffed with treats, puzzles and muffin tins with frozen goodies will keep you sane. Setting a timer will help you remember when you need to disassociate yourself from your work and spend quality time with your puppy. Play dog-soothing music to help your puppy learn to self-settle. Finding a doggie daycare or neighbor who can exercise your puppy in your absence can make all the difference to your puppy's well-being.

Most important, don't wait until the week before you return to an away-from-home schedule to teach your puppy these essential life skills. Planning ahead will mean your puppy will be well adjusted to your changing lifestyle.

Walking on a Leash/Heeling

This is an essential skill for most puppies and dogs any time they leave your home. This can also be a very difficult skill to teach and for your puppy to learn – the world is an interesting and exciting place, and we walk far too slowly for most puppies. Yes, we boring humans don't need to sniff every bush and chase every leaf.

First, have the right equipment. This includes an appropriately fitted collar, head or body harness, ID tag on the collar, comfortable leash and poop bags. Don't leave the collar on the puppy while in a crate or fenced yard if unsupervised, even for a minute. In a heartbeat, a collar can get caught on a fence or even the tooth of another dog, with a tragic outcome. Head harnesses are amazing tools for teaching a puppy to heel on leash, but must never be left on unless you are actively walking, even for the minute you stop to chat with your neighbor.

When putting the collar or head harness on, make it fun – but not so exciting that you can't contain the puppy's enthusiasm. If you have taught a reliable sit, have the puppy sit. Place the collar on the puppy and buckle it, then check to be sure it is neither too tight (two fingers should fit comfortably under it) nor so loose it will slip over the puppy's head if she backs away. If using a head harness, use a treat to lure the puppy's head through the nose loop, then buckle behind the ears.

Head harnesses are great tools, but can be a little tricky. The advantage is they give you control over the puppy's movements like a halter on a horse: Where their head goes, they go. Collars, on the other hand, are meant to be pulled against, which is why farmers use them on horses and cattle when they want them to pull a wagon. We use halters when we ride to have control over the head of a horse.

To be clear, a head halter is not a muzzle. Muzzles prevent a dog from opening his mouth. Head halters do not restrict opening the mouth – you can and should still give treats to a puppy that is wearing a head harness.

How do you put a head harness on? It looked easy when you got it and now on your own, it is like a puzzle! Check out YouTube if you are frustrated or need help.

76

There are two sets of straps – the short one on the D ring that goes over the nose in step one, and the long one with the buckle that goes around the dog's neck in step two. When you hold the head halter in both hands, with one hand on each strap, it makes a big "T" shape. Let go with one hand and push the short strap on the D ring up toward the ceiling, making the big "T" turn into a little "t." The loop of the little "t" creates the loop that goes over the muzzle. With a treat to entice your puppy, slip the little "t" loop over the muzzle. Then take the two long straps and buckle them behind the puppy's ears, assuring a correct fit of both loops. Both straps should be snug but not tight.

Start off on your walk immediately and briskly, not letting the puppy use her front feet to slip the nose loop off her muzzle. Don't stop to put on your jacket or pick up the mail or you will lose this first training experience – be ready before the head halter goes on.

At first, you may have a puppy who bucks a little, whether you're using a leash and collar or leash and head halter. A long-handled wooden spoon coated with peanut butter or soft cheese will allow you to get your puppy's attention. This has her focus on the treat and walking forward, rather than fighting the leash and collar/harness. Quickly, your puppy will learn to walk next to your knee. Most people, out of convention, have the dog walk on their left

DIG IT

Many dogs love to dig. They may dig in the garden, the couch or the middle of the good living-room carpet. Dogs who are "programmed" to be diggers can't help themselves. Just like a retriever retrieves, a terrier digs. You can't change Mother Nature. Instead of fighting your puppy's instincts, you can redirect them much more effectively.

Redirecting your puppy is best done by establishing a "digging pit" in an appropriate area of your yard. Use a substrate such as loose soil, sand or small pea gravel. Start by placing something interesting to your puppy in the area you have designated as the pit. Then partially bury the item. Keep making the item deeper and deeper. When your puppy starts to dig in the wrong area of the yard, patiently redirect her to the pit. With patience, and consistency, your puppy will have a great time in the yard, and your home will be safer for it.

GREETING VISITORS

Teaching your dog to lie belly down on a rug or mat a few feet from your door is a great tool when you have visitors stop by unexpectedly. The rug gives the dog a target to use to understand his boundary. The dog is close enough to the door for a stranger to see you have a "guard" dog and be part of the action. But the dog isn't charging out the door or jumping on your visitors.

What if you have an unwelcome, unwanted or threatening visitor? Release the dog from the down, keep your hand on the dog's collar and say, "I don't know how long I can hold him back." Only you will know the dog will lick your scary visitor to death. Use it to your advantage.

side, close to their knee, not behind or in front of them. But there is no reason you can't have a puppy on your right instead, or on either side if you want to teach both.

The important part is the puppy doesn't drag you and you don't drag the puppy. Most puppies don't start off heeling at your pace – you have to teach this. The younger you teach it, the better. As the puppy gets bigger, you will have a fight on your hands if you haven't taught this when he is little and happier to be at your side. The bigger the dog is going to get, the more important teaching this early is.

I don't recommend a choke chain or pinch collar, as this is "forceful" training. If you must use one of these devices, find someone who can help you use them as gently as possible.

Learning to walk/heel on a loose leash takes time and patience to teach. Remember, you are boring to your puppy. You need to keep moving fast enough and with the baited wooden spoon in front of your puppy's nose initially to keep his attention.

When you start off, use the spoon with the treat to get your puppy moving. Clearly, you can't keep the peanut butter going long enough to walk a mile. That's OK – your little puppy should not walk that far to start with. Puppies have tender footpads and growing bones, so be careful.

Once you are moving and lose the puppy's attention, you will need to do a fast-direction change. This is a quick, well-timed pivot. You will make quick 180-degree turns, with a varied number of steps before you pivot, with the dog on either the inside or outside of the turn. Once you swivel and the pup responds by moving back to your knee, praise the puppy. This will keep you from constantly popping the leash or dragging the dog. A tight leash will result in the dog opposing the correction, both mentally and physically. Rapid turning will throw the dog off, because you will become unpredictable in which direction you'll go next.

When you are not continuing in a straight line, the puppy will start to be more attentive, as you "cannot be relied on." He will need to keep an eye on you and will stop lunging in front of you. After a few pivots, you can continue along your straight path with a more attentive companion. Your neighbors will only think you are crazy for a minute. Be careful so you (or the child who is with you) doesn't get dizzy! This works better with your child/grandchild in a stroller or very stable wagon than on foot.

Bite Inhibition

Puppies, like small children, learn to experience the world with their mouths. Especially when excited, they tend to greet the world with open mouths. Even when they don't mean to, they often make contact with our delicate human skin. We don't have the thick hair coats and skin of our canine counterparts. So many times, our dogs catch us off guard, and inadvertently or intentionally catch our fragile skin with their teeth. When puppies are young, they don't have as much power in their jaws as they will when they are mature. But they have those tiny, sharp teeth that can damage our skin, clothing, shoelaces and other objects.

When puppies are young, we need to teach them a skill called "bite inhibition." There are many articles and publications that describe intentional contact of puppies' teeth with human skin as a training technique. I do NOT recommend this process, for many reasons. Instead, if and when this contact occurs, we can take this as an opportunity to train the pup to avoid contact with human skin. There are four steps to teaching this skill:

If or when a puppy contacts human skin, you should yelp, simulating the sound a puppy littermate would make if their sibling bit them too hard. This will generally startle the puppy, interrupting her biting. When small children or elderly family members are involved and likely to be snagged by your puppy's waggling teeth, you may need to be the source of the yelp. Practice making this yelping sound, which must be high-pitched, sharp and very brief to be effective.

CHEWING

Unfortunately, even before and long after teething is over, puppies chew. The only things you can do are puppy-proof the house, provide appropriate items to chew on, and supervise the puppy whenever he is not in a crate or X-pen. Without taking these steps, count on losing some of your prized possessions or having a new puppy end up at the veterinary clinic to treat a toxicity or in surgery to remove a foreign body.

During this brief respite, **stuff the puppy's open mouth with a soft chew toy.** This will redirect the puppy and given her a more appropriate outlet for her oral energy.

If the puppy continues to come at any human with an open mouth, **use a pillow or cushion as a "shield" for protection.**

If the puppy continues to show an overexuberance in the use of her open mouth, **quietly put the puppy in a "time out"** in her crate so she can calm down.

Teaching this skill is essential for all dogs and puppies, particularly large dogs or those with strong jaws such as terriers. Even a small amount of pressure in these breeds can cause serious damage to any human.

Dog teeth making contact with human skin is never acceptable. Although not ideal, dog-to-dog tooth contact is common. It is only a problem if the bites are serious enough to require veterinary care. Fortunately, in most multi-dog households, there may be a lot of scuffles involving growling and mouthing, but most of the time, it ends there. Just like people: We often raise our voices and argue, but we rarely send another human to the ER with an injury. Rarely, one or more dogs end up needing veterinary intervention.

It is completely unacceptable for an adult dog to contact human skin with his teeth, even if the skin isn't broken. As soon as this type of contact occurs, or you suspect it may occur, professional intervention is essential. Find a behaviorist with expertise in managing aggressive dogs and do it immediately. Once a dog bite occurs and requires medical intervention, the law becomes involved. A police officer or sheriff is likely to show up at your door within 24 hours of an emergency-room visit. In most states, a biting dog is a dead dog. Because insurance companies can't accept a client who has a dog with a bite history, you will either lose your dog or lose your insurance. Intervene with a certified behaviorist immediately!

Recall

A reliable recall is an essential skill for your puppy to learn, second only to an **emergency down**.

Like sits and downs, recalls can be taught to even very young puppies. When puppies are under four months of age, recalls are easy – puppies want to be with you. There are fewer distractions at this age, as they only have social interests. However, once a puppy reaches four months, the world opens up, and she sees and hears things at a distance that she didn't when she was younger, making recalls a thing of the past.

Start young and practice many times a day.

Key steps are:

- Start with **rewarding eye contact,** the first step toward getting your puppy's attention.

- Use an **attention-getting sound, not a word**, while teaching this cue. Everyone in the family should use the same sound. Make it one that little children and adult men can make uniformly.

- Only work with the puppy on this when on a **long line**, so if there is a failure to come, you can "reel" the puppy in. Don't trust your puppy any time you are not in a secure area.

- If you have the bad fortune to have the puppy off leash and need him to come, **run in the opposite direction while calling your puppy.** Chasing will prompt him to run away from you.

- **Have a really wonderful treat ready** for the puppy when he comes when called. And give it to him – don't just tease him with it.

- **Vary the treats** to keep it interesting. Remember the difference between lures, rewards and bribes. (See page 62.)

- **Don't vary the recall word** – consistency among all trainers is essential. Only change the word if you have mistakenly taught the wrong one. "Come," "here" or any term that makes sense is OK to use.

- **Attach a term once the puppy has learned the skill.** Only use the word once.

- **Practice throughout the day**, over and over, in different places with different distractions. Puppies are situational, not generalized, learners. This means the puppy cannot apply a lesson learned in one context to another. Be specific on teaching him what you want him to learn.

- **Don't make the recall become the end of a fun activity**, or the puppy will begin to dread it. In other words, call the puppy, then release her to go play again as soon as she comes and gets the treat. Don't use the recall as a way to catch the puppy and stuff her into her crate.

- No matter what, when the puppy comes, **always make it a positive reunion.** Even when you are frustrated by your puppy's shenanigans, praise her and treat her when she returns.

Down

This is a very useful command to teach a puppy as soon as possible: You can't get into too much trouble if you are lying down. You can't jump on grandma or the grandkids. You can't run out the front door that was left ajar. You can't steal food off the countertops or kitchen table.

Remember, "down" is different than "off." "Down" means to lie down with your belly on the floor. "Off" means stop jumping up. Don't confuse the puppy with conflicting expectations.

Teaching down can be lots of fun. It will likely require you to get down on the floor. Getting down isn't usually the hard part for most of us; it's getting back up that creates the issue. Make sure a chair is nearby to stabilize yourself when you rise.

Using a food treat as a lure, direct the puppy from a sit (that you have taught or have lured the puppy into), then direct the food treat downward between his front feet. Some puppies are "tuckers" and some are "folders"; in other words, some lean back, while some drop straight into a down. Either one is acceptable as long as he puts his belly on the floor.

If this doesn't work for you and your puppy, sit on the floor with your foot on a wall, door or solid piece of furniture (like a couch) with your calf parallel with the floor. With the puppy on one side of you, use a food treat to lure the puppy to crawl under your leg and out the other side. Repeat as often as you can.

Gradually, teach the puppy to stay in a down position longer and longer. Then put him on a down/stay command with a word, once mastered.

Emergency Down

This one training technique is the single most life-saving technique you can teach your dog. Start when your puppy is still young. After you have taught "down," start teaching the puppy to "down" as you step farther and farther away. You may need to teach this with the puppy on one side of the gate and you on the other as you advance. Or you may need a second person to help you.

A great hand signal for this is to raise your hand over your head as the visual cue. Remember to use the word *after* the puppy understands what "down" is.

Why do you need an "emergency down"?

Because if your puppy slips away, crosses the road, and turns to come back to you while a semi-truck is cruis-

OFF THE FURNITURE

In general, puppies and adult dogs should not be allowed on the furniture, bed or other high objects without being invited for several reasons:

- **Status.** In the dog world, being higher or taller means status. You and your family should have the highest status in the home, with the puppy ranking lower. Only allow the dog to be on the furniture when invited.

- **Injury.** Too many puppies fall or are dropped off the furniture, which can cause injuries, including fractured limbs. That is expensive to fix and painful for your puppy.

- **Damage to your belongings.** If the puppy is on the good recliner, she is more likely to either urinate or chew it up. Keeping her on the floor with appropriate chew toys is safer.

"DROP IT" OR "GIVE IT"

Tug of war games are NOT recommended by most dog professionals out of concern that they can become a game of wills. Dog-to-dog tug of war is OK if you don't mind having a winner become more assertive toward the losing dog. However, in human-dog tug of war, if the dog either initiates or finishes, even if it is because you quit when you got bored, the dog comes out the winner. This is where you will get into trouble. Best advice is avoid these games altogether.

"Drop it" or "Give it" is a completely different game, if you are careful. This starts when the

dog is racing through the house with your new lingerie, the baby's pacifier (a great bowel obstruction waiting to happen) or a remote control. The trick is to have the dog learn to bring it to you and relinquish your item without damage. To do this, the dog gets to trade his newfound unmentionable with a high-value treat, something really yummy. By doing this, the dog will learn to come to you with what he has, instead of taking off the other way every time you get within finger's length from him. Remember, the faster you try to take away his goodie, the faster he will try to swallow it. As with other training, start young. Make it fun. And be consistent.

Better yet, don't give the dog access to items you want off limits. But we all slip up and leave the toddler's Legos® out or drop a pill on the floor. We can't all live in Felix's apartment from "The Odd Couple"; sometimes we are Oscar.

ing down the road between the two of you, calling "come" guarantees your puppy will end up as a grease spot on the road.

Because if Grandma comes over to visit, and your Great Dane jumps on her, she will end up in the ER.

Because if the kids are running through the yard with hot dogs in their hands, and your puppy decides a fun game to play is "take the hot dog away from the child," you can intervene with an emergency down before the child swings his hand over his head and your dog unintentionally removes part of his ear.

Why do you need an "emergency down"? Because ... You fill in the blank here. The above scenarios all happened to beloved dogs belonging to my clients.

Why use a raised hand over your head? It is easy to see from across the highway. It is a natural move when a child is running with a hot dog. It is a quick reaction you can learn.

Just teach it. Hopefully you will never have your own "I saved my dog" story. But if you do, you and your dog will both come out winners.

Omega Roll

This is a great tool for you to use at home and for veterinary exams. In this procedure, you ask the puppy to roll onto her side or back, without force. When on her side or upside down, you can pull gum or burdocks out of her coat, treat a torn toenail, or your veterinarian can do an ultrasound or staple a wound without sedation. This takes practice, so don't start teaching it the day before you go in for a veterinary visit. And make it really fun.

Start with a treat over your puppy's nose, luring her into a sit. Then, move the treat back toward the hip that she is not putting her weight on. This moves her into a C shape. Continue to move the treat farther over her rear, until she drops and positions herself belly up. Reward with the treat you used to lure her. Some dogs prefer going to the same side every time. That's OK.

This is an "omega" roll – meaning you teach your puppy to do this willingly. It is not forced; it is voluntary and trained. It is not a way to shake your puppy up and dominate her – what is sometimes called an "alpha roll." Once you have the maneuver trained, you can use a fun cue like "play dead" or a similar command.

The time you take to do this now will pay you back many times over when your puppy is happily being examined for skin lesions or lumps at the veterinary clinic.

Stand for Exam

This also is a great "trick" to teach your puppy for veterinary visits. Using the word "stand" after your puppy is standing still, use a food treat. Quietly give the treat to keep him from getting too excited. Have the puppy continue to stand on all four feet for a short time. Slowly increase the time and distractions. Include teaching the puppy to allow his ears, mouth or feet to be examined. Again, this will teach your puppy handling skills that will make him a rock star at the veterinary clinic. This can save you time and money, as he won't need sedation for minor exams and procedures.

Of course, if the puppy has a serious health problem and needs to be more completely relaxed, don't feel like a failure. Exams can be hard to tolerate, even for humans who understand the reason for procedures. Sometimes sedation or anesthesia is best for a complete exam and for your and the puppy's mental well-being.

Attention-Seeking Behavior

While pawing, nudging under your elbow, or barking at you can be cute in a puppy, it loses its charm when the dog is an adult. Just like kids who act up when you are on the telephone, puppies learn quickly when you are too preoccupied to attend to their needs. The best way to manage this is to have an appropriate chew toy stuffed, frozen and ready to deploy when the phone rings or the Zoom call starts.

Traveling

Before you take off for the cross-country family vacation, practice short car rides. This allows the puppy to get the hang of travel. Include learning to go potty on leash in unfamiliar surroundings. Start young. Additionally, if you find your puppy needs medication for anxiety and/or nausea, you can obtain it from your veterinarian and try it out before traveling to nail the correct dose. During COVID-19 and its aftermath, more and more families are taking road trips and camping. More dogs will be able to join them. Don't forget the puppy's sunscreen, insect-bite repellent, and flea and tick meds.

If needed, maropitant (Cerenia®) is a prescription medication to help minimize car sickness. Anti-anxiety medications can be used, particularly for trips to the veterinarian, groomer or long distance.

Don't forget your puppy in the car! Every year dogs accidentally left in the car in moderate weather become an extreme emergency.

If you run into the house for the grocery list or into the store for just a minute, remember the car can get very hot very fast. The best thing to do is hang your puppy's leash over your shoulders when you leave the car. By doing this, you will remember that you left him in the car when the phone rings during your quick trip inside. It is also a great idea to have a window sticker with your cell phone number on it. That way, a Good Samaritan who comes across your vehicle with your dog inside can call you, rather than break a window.

When you take your dog out of your parked car, it is a great idea to leave your crate doors off or open in the unoccupied vehicle so it is obvious to well-meaning passersby that the crates are unoccupied and no dogs are in danger.

Teaching "Touch"

Teaching your pup a "touch" technique is a great tool. Start by teaching your pup to touch his nose to your hand, a wooden spoon or small plate. Once the pup learns touch, you can use it to lead him through other training. He can learn to slow down and touch as he comes off the dog walk in agility. He can push the refrigerator door closed after you get out a drink. He can touch the bell at the door to ask to go out to go potty. He can close the door from the garage as you carry in the groceries. You will constantly be surprised by what your puppy learns, if you just keep him engaged.

CHAPTER 8

Separation and Generalized Anxiety

You and your dog have become very tight during the pandemic: She follows you to the bathroom. She sits next to you on the couch while you eat dinner. She is your shadow, and you love having her with you. She knows your every move and emotion, reading you better than the people you are close to. This is a great relationship – one you have been longing for.

But one day, you realize she is picking up on cues that you are preparing to leave home without her. At first, it's kind of cute as she watches you shut down your computer, then put on the shoes you wear when you are going someplace where she can't join you; she knows which shoes are the "fun" ones you wear on walks and trips to the dog park. Then you notice she is more animated during this departure routine.

Before you know it, she has started showing signs of emotional distress. She won't go into her crate when you are leaving. She is increasingly agitated. Then you hear from your neighbor that she barked for 15 minutes after you drove away. Next you come home to a crate soaked with

SIGNS OF ANXIETY

- Pacing

- Vocalizing inappropriately for a prolonged period

- Salivating and/or panting excessively

- Sweaty foot pads

- Trembling and/or shaking

- Failure to eat, drink or chew on toys as your dog normally would

- Destructive behavior that is out of character

- Inappropriate urination and/or defecation

- Evidence of desperate attempts to escape the crate or home

- Other signs that look like the puppy is having a panic attack

saliva from her panting. Its bars are starting to become misshapen from her escape attempts. She was always good with housebreaking, but now is messing in the house. And though before she never chewed anything, now you are afraid to return home for fear of finding yet another valuable personal item destroyed. And the big bowl of food or treat-stuffed toy you left her with to keep her happy? It hasn't been touched – she waits until you walk in the door to start eating.

With our additional time working and schooling from home, our dogs have become accustomed to this new "normal" routine. There are no after-work stops for drinks with co-workers, no athletic events for the kids after school, no running out for dinner. We have spent this time walking our puppy four times a day. We have been hanging out on the couch, binge-watching TV with him at our feet.

During the pandemic, we've seen more dogs rehomed through foster and rescue groups. These dogs are at increased risk of separation anxiety. Add to this the great experience they have had with you being home, enjoying the extra attention. Unfortunately, once working or schooling from home is minimized or ended, these dogs risk entering into an emotional crisis.

If you believe your dog or puppy is at risk, make a preemptive strike. Start training her to adapt to your upcoming schedule changes and work with your veterinarian, trainer and others to keep this disorder from sneaking up on you and your dog. And if your dog is starting to show symptoms, for her sake and yours, ask for help from a qualified veterinary professional sooner rather than later.

What is separation anxiety?

Separation anxiety is the behavior of a pet when left alone without his preferred person as a companion. This is a panic disorder, a serious problem. Separation anxiety starts before you leave the dog home (or wherever you are leaving him) and does not end until you return or shortly after your return. It can manifest as simple anxiety symptoms such as pacing, panting and restlessness, or can escalate into serious destructive behavior. It can become so severe you may be concerned for your dog's safety.

Separation anxiety is a common form of anxiety in the dog. It is distressing to most owners because they don't want their pet to be upset by their absence. It is also worrisome because of the risk of injury to their pet and the destruction of their home that can occur. This is not the garden variety of chewing up items in your home or recreational barking. It is a true panic/anxiety disorder that is associated with your impending or current absence, leaving the dog in a state of panic.

Separation anxiety is different from ...

... generalized anxiety. Dogs with generalized anxiety constantly live under a little black cloud, like Pig-Pen from the Peanuts cartoon. Separation anxiety is expressed when your dog's favorite person is out of range. With generalized anxiety, many dogs experience angst, even when their favorite person is with them. Trips to the vet or groomer, thunderstorms and fireworks, strangers in the home, a package delivered to the front door — anything out of the norm or that is noisy can cause anxiety.

... training issues, including poor manners, downright naughtiness (which can take a decade or longer to outgrow) and dogs that haven't been housebroken or trained to leave things alone.

... environmental issues, including homes that are not dog-proofed, dogs left unattended for too long, and dogs that need to be crated when alone until they outgrow immature behaviors

The importance of determining the reason for your dog's unfortunate behavior is clear: We need a diagnosis to accurately treat these behaviors. Some will respond to environmental changes, some to behavioral counseling, and some to medication. Most need a combination of all three.

Even puppies can show early signs of not coping well when one or more favorite people are inaccessible to them. This can mean that even if you are home but in another part of the house, your puppy becomes anxious.

Preventing Separation Anxiety

Like most behavioral conditions, separation anxiety is easier to prevent than to manage. Curing it may require the assistance of a professional dog trainer as well as medications. It can take a very long time to manage and see improvement.

Prevention should start the day you bring your new puppy home. The best way to prevent separation anxiety is to teach your puppy or new dog to be without you for short periods of time and to self-soothe. This may not be easy, as some dogs have an inherent tendency to have generalized anxiety and therefore are also prone to developing separation anxiety.

On a daily basis, start leaving your puppy alone in her crate for short periods with you out of sight. Offer a treat-stuffed toy or other suitable, safe "lovie" toy. Slowly increase the time the puppy is alone. A radio, sound machine, doggie TV station or dog-music CD will help cover up background noise. Over time, the puppy can practice self-soothing, learning to stay relaxed when home alone.

Making a big production about leaving the house can contribute to separation anxiety. Learn how to leave and return quietly and quickly without dramatic goodbyes and baby talk. You can greet your dog lovingly and kindly when arriving home without creating too much drama. Drama at these times will increase the odds your new dog will develop separation anxiety.

Once we start to return to our former routines, we'll need to help our dogs transition to new patterns. You'll need to restructure the schedule he is accustomed to by teaching him to be comfortable in a crate. Start leaving him alone for short periods of time, very slowly increasing the time alone. Be sure he is not alone for too long, using neighbors or pet sitters for trips outside if you're delayed getting home. Make certain your puppy has plenty to do to stay busy in your absence with safe, durable toys stuffed with food treats. With care in teaching your puppy to be comfortable home alone, you can prevent separation anxiety from developing.

Don't wait to start this until you and your family are going back to work and school. It will take time for your puppy or dog to learn how to comfortably be left alone.

What is going on while she is home alone?

Separation anxiety is commonly seen in puppies with first-time owners. As a new dog owner, you want to bond with your puppy or dog, and often go overboard in developing a strong relationship. This is not something you should be embarrassed to discuss with a trainer and your veterinarian, as it is likely to require both to work through.

If you suspect your dog is developing or has separation anxiety, the most effective diagnostic tool is to place a video camera in the area of your home where your dog spends his time in your absence. Like security cameras, these can be watched remotely or can archive video so you can observe your dog's behavior without his awareness. It is important that you distinguish between generalized anxiety, training issues (a puppy left without the skills required for being alone), environmental issues (a house with too many opportunities to get into trouble) and the true panic attacks characteristic of separation anxiety.

Additionally, it's been my experience based on the dogs I see in veterinary practice that there are increased numbers of dogs placed by rescue organizations showing signs of all types of anxiety, both separation and generalized. The reasons are unknown, but possibly this group of dogs has increased risk of anxiety disorder because of unknown genetics and socialization, multiple moves during the critical social period puppies go through, and the likelihood of emotional trauma while pups are developing.

Separation anxiety was once described as a rare behavior problem in dogs. It now accounts for 20 to 40 percent of cases seen by veterinary behaviorists. It's likely even more common than that.

Separation anxiety may be underreported because owners may not recognize its symptoms. For instance, I have a lot of clients who say, "She doesn't eat while I am gone from the house" or "He doesn't drink while I am work because he knows he can't get out to go potty while I am gone." We think dogs are smart, but I don't think they are smart enough to know that drinking more means more urine in their bladder.

Many dogs also have mild enough symptoms – like not eating or drinking when separated from their favorite person – or are not destructive enough to warrant attention or treatment by their veterinarian or veterinary behaviorist.

Another reason for underreporting separation anxiety is many owners try finding their own solutions such as herbal preparations, CBD oil (*not* recommended) or Benadryl® (an antihistamine, not an anti-anxiety drug). If you want to try an herbal preparation, choose carefully. Herbsmith, based out of Oconomowoc, Wisconsin, is owned by Eastern-trained veterinarian Dr. Christine Bessant, who provides the science behind her products. Be very careful when choosing products not tested and approved as safe by the FDA.

Finally, owners may be reluctant to share this problem with their veterinary professional. They may feel intimidated, embarrassed or be unaware that their veterinary team can assist with this concern.

Generalized Anxiety

Many dogs, particularly those who have unknown heritage or have had multiple attempts at finding their forever home, including rescue dogs, live their lives in a constant state of generalized anxiety. Even if you don't have anxieties of your own, you can imagine this is no way to live.

These dogs need help. Anti-anxiety medication can help them learn to deal with their anxieties, but most need additional desensitization and training to cope with their stressors.

Management and Treatment of Anxiety

If you suspect your dog has either generalized anxiety or separation anxiety, and your best efforts to prevent or manage anxiety have failed, seek the help of a professional veterinary behaviorist and appropriate medication. These two steps can make the difference between a dog you can rehabilitate and manage and a dog that you cannot keep safe in your home and you cannot keep your home safe from.

Remember, some dogs who have generalized anxiety may also have separation anxiety and vice versa. Dogs with a tendency to have anxiety are likely to be predisposed to both types. The good news is that the medications we use for anxiety will work for both, as long as we use long-acting medications. The rest of the good news is that using behavior modification for anxiety and desensitizing our dogs to stressful situations will allow them to learn to soothe themselves. Medications can allow your dog to more rapidly learn how to manage his emotions and behaviors.

- **Reduce the drama when you leave and return home.** You shouldn't feel or act guilty about leaving your dog home when you go to work, school or run errands. These trips are necessary. If you are calm departing and returning, your dog will pick up on your cues that this is part of the routine and no big deal. Without a job, you can't provide for those wonderful treats, a nice home and the veterinary care your puppy needs.

- **Give your dog the tools she needs to self-soothe and stay out of trouble in your absence.** Help her acclimate to being in a crate or small, safe room slowly, when you are home with her. Teach her to look forward to the muffin tin with her breakfast kibble frozen in yogurt when you depart in the morning. Provide appropriate chew toys in a safe environment. Set your dog up for success. You may need to confine your dog in a safe space for more than a year, so plan accordingly and make it pleasant for her.

MEDICATIONS FOR ANXIETY

There are two general categories of medications that can be used to help with different forms of anxiety, regardless of whether your puppy has generalized or separation anxiety:

Short-term episodes of anxiety, such as trips to the vet or groomer, thunderstorms and/or fireworks. This includes drugs such as alprazolam, valium, gabapentin, trazodone and Sileo®.

Long-term generalized anxiety, including separation anxiety and the angst of our pets in dealing with everyday stressors. Controls include drugs such as fluoxetine (Prozac®), clomipramine (Clomicalm®), paroxetine (Paxil®) and sertraline (Zoloft®).

The need to use medications while you are also using behavioral modification to help your pet through these fearful episodes should not be anything to be embarrassed about. Rather, use of meds should be a sign of the love you have for your pet and your appreciation for his well-being.

Keep in mind that Benadryl® and acepromazine are not anti-anxiety medications. They may immobilize your pet, giving you the impression she is "calm," but in reality, the dog is frozen in place and still terrified.

Our pets should not suffer with anxiety of any type. Medications may be used for long-term solutions, but are often useful in helping pets "relearn" how to deal with life. Over the course of time, dogs can often be weaned off medications. Always consult with your veterinary professional before altering medication doses up or down, or discontinuing them. Be certain you only use medications prescribed by your veterinarian. Do not administer your medications to your pets.

- **Teach your dog "counter-conditioning."** Work hard to create a positive emotional state for him prior to your departure. Your dog can be helped to look forward to your departure, so he can get on with his busy day of slowly munching on his stuffed hollow toy.

Each dog has its own formula for figuring out you are leaving without him. For some it is the work shoes you don, instead of the "fun" shoes. For others, it is keys or jackets. Or it might be clicking the TV off with the remote or closing down your computer. By close observation, you can unravel your dog's triggers or cues that you are preparing to leave. Once you have assessed what he picks up on, you can get to work on "desensitizing" or "counter-conditioning" him, so he is reprogrammed to accept your calm departure.

This desensitization process can take time, so make a list of triggers and a schedule for the process. The key step is to acclimate your dog to you walking out the door, and have him remain calm for the first 10 minutes you are gone and the last 10 minutes before you return (if you have a set schedule). These time ranges represent when most dogs show signs of the panic attack known as separation anxiety.

By changing how your dog "feels" about you leaving and the associated triggers, you can reduce the risk of the destructive or inappropriate behaviors he exhibits.

To do this, you need to distract your dog with his favorite food or toy while you "pretend" to leave, performing the activities he associates with your departure. In advance, let him see you stuff his favorite hollow safe toy. Let him have the toy briefly, perform the triggering behavior, and in a split second, take the toy away. Repeat by giving him the toy, perform the trigger, and take away the toy again. After several repetitions, put the toy in the fridge, and go about your daily activities without leaving the area where he is hanging out.

This activity allows your dog to learn to look forward to your triggering behavior instead of dreading it. Repeat this daily. As you progress, add additional steps he associates with your departure to the trigger, to continue desensitizing him to being alone.

After he becomes more relaxed with this routine, start to leave for very brief periods, at first barely taking your hand off the doorknob. Then, over time, leave for extended periods of time, with very short time increments at the beginning. Over time, you can leave for longer and longer periods, but not going too fast at first.

- **Avoid punishment for destruction you find on arrival home.** Coming home to damage is upsetting. But punishment after the fact will only create more angst the next time you leave. Your dog can't understand that what happened earlier in the day was her fault, so avoid losing your cool. By housing her in a crate or pen when unsupervised, you can minimize damage. Leaving a puppy home, loose in the house, will predictably lead to destruction, so prevent that from happening. You would not leave a 2-year-old child home alone, so don't do the same to yourself and your new puppy.

Non-Pharmaceutical Options for Anxiety

- **Pheromones** – A form of hormonal communication. These biological messaging tools occur naturally, such as the comforting messages mother dogs release to their puppies during birth and lactation. These odorless pheromones have been synthesized in labs to help with dog and cat behavior (Adaptil® for dogs, Feliway® for cats). Other species, including humans, are not affected.

  Pheromones come in several forms – sprays, collars and room atomizers. They are not used internally like a drug. They have been met with variable success, but can be useful in the right circumstance for the right dog.

  The company that manufactures Adaptil® has research to show its Junior collar will help your puppy sleep through the night within five days, help your puppy play and learn more, and be less fearful.

- **Thundershirts** – These actual shirts apply gentle, constant pressure over your puppy's trunk to help reduce anxiety, fearfulness and overexcitement, similar to the effect of swaddling a baby. They can be used during thunderstorms, travel, fireworks and periods of separation. Neither pheromones nor Thundershirts are a substitute for training or acclimating your puppy to new situations.

- **CBD oil and essential oils** – At the time of this writing, there are no studies to show safety or efficacy of these products in any form.

- **Doggie day care** – You may be able to find a doggie daycare near your home, school or workplace. Some provide training as well as a place to spend the day. Or you may find a neighbor who doesn't want the responsibility of full-time dog care but would love to spend some daytime hours with your dog.

- **Fear Free Happy Homes** (www.fearfreepets.com) includes many resources, articles and videos.

Dr. Patricia McConnell has an outstanding short book about how to prevent and manage separation anxiety called "I'll Be Home Soon!" If you are still struggling with what you believe is separation anxiety, you may wish to purchase a copy or download it to speed you and your dog in working through this painful but rewarding recovery.

Need more help?

Work with a certified animal behaviorist or your veterinary professional. You can find highly skilled veterinary professionals at the American College of Veterinary Behaviorists, or ACVB, website (www.dacvb.org). This is the certifying board for veterinarians who are specially trained to advance the behavioral health of animals through clinical practice, research and science-based behavior education. You can find veterinarians with expertise in managing dog behavior in your area using this resource.

CHAPTER 9

Feeding and Grooming

Selecting the primary diet you feed your puppy is one of the most important decisions for her health you can make. Because she will be fed twice daily for her lifetime, this decision should be carefully researched and evaluated.

Be certain to discuss your puppy or dog's nutrition and treats with your veterinary professional so you are certain you are feeding her appropriately. Food and water are essential to your puppy's good health.

What and How to Feed

I recommend feeding three meals a day to puppies under six months of age, and then two meals a day after they reach six months and for the rest of their lives.

Housebreaking is much easier if you feed regular meals; puppies that eat on a schedule will be more reliable on when they need to have a stool. Put the measured amount of dry food into a bowl and give the puppy access to that meal for no more than 30 minutes. If she finishes her meal, take her outside immediately. If she doesn't eat everything, pick the food up and save it for the next meal. If you added canned food or other toppings, refrigerate the food until the next meal. Warming refrigerated food covered in the microwave will help the food be more appealing.

Selecting Your Puppy's Food

There are literally thousands of puppy and dog food diets on the market. Making the decision of what to feed can be very confusing. What and how much you feed your puppy and dog as he matures will make a huge difference in his health, stool, weight and longevity.

The best sources of information on pet food are:

Your veterinarian – Yes, your veterinarian did take classes on nutrition. For the record, veterinarians do *not* get "kickbacks" from the pet-food industry. They may sell pet food, but these are like loss leaders at the grocery store when they sell milk for $1.69 – it is not a profit center for veterinarians to sell pet food. Your veterinarian and her veterinary team know the foods that are manufactured locally and nationally. Ask what they feed their own dogs.

Your breeder – Although most breeders don't have a nutrition background, they know what diet agrees with their dogs. Some also sell dog food and may make a profit from it, so choose carefully.

FORMS OF FOOD ON THE MARKET

- Kibble or dry
- Canned or wet
- Fresh refrigerated
- Frozen
- Freeze dried
- Semi-moist in pouches
- Homemade

Is kibble OK?

Absolutely. I recommend dry kibble for most puppies from one of the big three pet food manufacturers: Purina, Hill's Science Diet and Royal Canin/Iams/Eukanuba (Mars). I recommend these foods because these are the companies with science behind their diets. Many food companies put their money into marketing, not research. These big three pet-food companies spend their money on researching and developing diets that improve our pets' health. They also spend their money on feeding trials – feeding dogs and cats in their highly specialized facilities to ensure the foods they formulate are ideal to support the special life stage your dog is in. Many of the other diet companies formulate diets they want you to believe contain better ingredients. Pet foods should not be assessed on ingredients, but on their nutrient profiles. Many of these contain excesses or inadequate amounts of nutrients.

Kibble has many advantages: It is affordable, quick, easy and a balanced meal that you can't easily manage with homemade or raw-meat diets.

READING LABELS

Ingredients on dog-food labels don't tell the whole story, as this information can be manipulated. Trying to understand the AAFCO analysis is also confusing. If you have questions about diets, call the 800 number on the bag and talk to their representatives. Ask if they have a *veterinary* nutritionist on staff. Use the unbiased information on the World Small Animal Veterinary Association website: https://wsava.org/wp-content/uploads/2020/01/Selecting-the-Best-Food-for-your-Pet.pdf. This website has excellent guidelines and questions to ask to help you assess your dog's food needs.

What about raw-meat diets?

Most veterinary professionals do not endorse the feeding of raw-meat or grain-free diets. Raw-meat diets carry the risk of introducing bacteria (*Salmonella*, *Shigella*, *E. coli* and others) and parasites (Toxoplasmosis and Neosporum) into your kitchen and environment as you interact with your dog. Many of these diets are not nutritionally complete.

Some owners wish to make homemade diets. While you may start off with a balanced diet based on a verified recipe, most people end up with "recipe drift" where the ingredients slowly change over time. Again, this often leads to an incomplete or unbalanced diet. This may mean either a deficiency of some nutrients, or, just as important, some nutrients may be present in too large a quantity.

I see too many little dogs who eat chicken breasts as their only diet. This is clearly not nutritionally complete and balanced. If your dog needs a homemade or custom diet, or you choose this route for feeding your pet, consult with a qualified veterinary nutritionist. One source that can help you formulate an appropriate diet is https://secure.balanceit. com/recipegenerator_ver4/index.php?rotator=EZ. Very few pet owners can formulate a balanced diet for their pet's homemade diets without the professional assistance of a veterinary nutritionist.

A programmable pressure-cooker/slow-cooker combination appliance like the Instant Pot is a great tool to use if you choose to do some home cooking for your dog. This allows you to quickly and safely cook meats such as poultry as well as make homemade yogurt that you can share with your puppy.

What about grain-free diets?

In the past couple of years, grain-free diets have come under scrutiny. Initially, a grain-free diet was promoted as a healthier food choice for our dogs. It seems it came along with the gluten-free craze on the human-nutrition side.

While grain-free diets can be a good solution for the very small percentage of dogs who appear to have food sensitivities or food allergies, they are not superior nutritionally for non-allergic dogs.

In 2018, grain-free diets were linked to dilated cardiomyopathy (DCM) in some dogs. While not all grain-free diets were implicated, and not all dogs appeared to be equally affected by this heart condition, the concern was still real. Even now, the veterinary community still doesn't have all the answers. It appears dogs with DCM have one or more of three underlying causes – genetic, nutritional and unknown. Golden Retrievers and other breeds with a genetic predisposition, such as Doberman Pinschers, Great Danes and Boxers, should particularly avoid grain-free diets and/or have blood taurine levels tested.

Since we still don't have all of the answers we need, most veterinary professionals recommend avoiding feeding a grain-free or gluten-free diet pending more answers. This may save your dog's life. It certainly will save you money. Unless your veterinarian has prescribed a grain-free or similar diet, avoid feeding grain-free diets until we know more.

> ## What about other small-producer diets?

There are too many diets on the market to assess each one. Some very good products are manufactured by small, regional pet-food companies. Discuss your nutritional questions about your specific dog with your veterinary professional to be certain you are making the best choice possible.

Water

Water is often overlooked as the most important nutrient your dog needs. Be certain your puppy has access to a clean water source in a clean bowl (ceramic, stainless steel or glass) that is washed daily to remove slobber and slime.

Many people want to offer constant access to water for their puppies. This may make you feel better, but it can make housebreaking more difficult. One great middle-ground solution is to offer water in a drinking bottle in the puppy's crate. Lixit makes several different-sized bottles that have the advantage of water access without allowing the puppy to drink excessively, drink the bowl dry, or turn her crate into a swimming pool. This type of bottle has a metal tip with a ball in the end – similar but larger than what you give gerbils for their water source. You can teach the puppy to use the drinking bottle by smearing peanut butter, liver sausage or soft cheese on the tip, and letting her learn by exploring and licking it.

Offering water, like meals, in pre-dosed quantities and at convenient times will allow you to better predict when you need to take your puppy outside to go potty.

Fast Eaters

One way you can occupy your puppy or prevent her from gulping down her meals is by feeding in a metal muffin tin. You can place a dab of peanut butter or soft cheese in the muffin tin, press a gingersnap flat side down into the bottom of each well, and let your puppy go at it. You can also fill it with yogurt and dog kibble and freeze. A metal muffin tin filled with treats and topped off with a tennis ball in each well will keep your puppy busy.

Alternatively, to slow the chowing down, you can use a slow feeder or puzzle (there are many on the market) or a roasting pan to spread out the meal. Avoid using silicone muffin tins or silicone mats, as pieces of these can be ingested when unsupervised.

Treats

Treats are a hot topic for many owners. Some feel strongly that "people" food is a bad idea. However, there are many treats people eat that work very well as training treats for our dogs. Others are not safe for them.

Many commercial dog treats are expensive, high in sodium, and can deliver a remarkably high calorie count, leading to obesity. Using human food for treats is perfectly acceptable as long as the treats don't exceed 10 percent of your puppy's daily food and calorie intake.

And if you don't feed from the table or breadboard, your pet will not "know" the treat is human food. So, relax – it's OK to use the following items.

- **Cheese, cooked chicken and cooked liver** are great training treats. Using these allows you to control what your dog is eating.

- **Hot dogs** – Cut in quarters the long way, then into tiny bites. Microwave on a paper towel until the consistency of pepperoni. You can keep these in a bag in your jacket pocket at the door. Hang it high enough so the puppy won't chew a hole in the pocket of the jacket you keep the treats in.

- **Fresh and frozen fruits and vegetables** (except grapes, raisins, onions, large amounts of garlic and macadamia nuts) are excellent for your pets. Short-cut carrots, lettuce, most fruits and vegetables, and frozen green beans are great snacks for your puppy. Introduce these when the puppy is young. These treats are low-calorie, high fiber, not highly processed, high in antioxidants and can take a long time to munch on. They can be used to keep your puppy busy, to supplement his diet or as training treats.

- **Cheerios** – Plain or your preferred flavor. There are three Cheerios to a calorie. (Really, I counted them.)

- **Liquid smoke to flavor treats** – You can find this in the grilling department at superstores. By sealing treats, like Cheerios, in an airproof container and adding a few drops of liquid smoke, you can make delicious, low-cal treats for your dog.

- **Gingersnaps** – Yes, the human cookies. A great snack that will help your puppy's stomach be more settled during travel.

- **"Stuffable" toys** can be filled with soft and spray cheese, liver sausage, peanut butter and yogurt. These are great toys to leave with your pet to keep him busy in your absence or when you are otherwise distracted. Once stuffed, they can be frozen so your puppy will be busy for a long time.

Grooming

All dogs, regardless of breed, size, age or lifestyle, need good basic hygiene care to remain healthy. Time spent teaching your young puppy how to be comfortable during these important grooming events will pay off with a happier dog and lower grooming costs. Handling your puppy gently so he becomes accustomed to basic hygiene is important. Starting when your puppy first arrives home, you can acclimate him to the basics of grooming care. This includes coat care, bathing, nail trims, ear care and dental care. Your veterinary professionals and groomers will appreciate a puppy that accepts the mechanics of handling. Not only will your puppy be less stressed at his appointments if he is relaxed during handling, but it will also cost you less over the course of his lifetime.

Coat Care

The care you need to provide your puppy is highly dependent on the breed of dog you have and the purpose of the dog. A show Standard Poodle will have much different coat-care needs than a Goldendoodle.

Longer-coated dogs that don't shed and are not being shown at dog shows will need a trip to the groomer every six to eight weeks for clipping and bathing. Dogs that do shed and have short coats, like Labrador Retrievers, may never see a groomer and may only need a bath after rolling on something dead and smelly.

It's a good idea to have an appropriate shampoo available in case you need to do an emergency bath. Use dog shampoo, not human shampoo. Dawn dish soap can be used if it is necessary to degrease or decontaminate your puppy's coat if she gets into something oily or toxic. Most dogs should not be bathed more often than every six weeks unless the dog has a skin condition and you have been advised to use medicated shampoo by your veterinarian.

SELECTING A GROOMER

Selecting a groomer is a lot like selecting a veterinarian or a dog-training class. Ask your friends and neighbors for recommendations. Ask your veterinarian for a recommendation. Stop in for a visit. Ask about their procedures and processes. Do they have an assistant? How long do they need your dog for? Do they work on more than one dog at a time? Does your dog seem happy to go in? Anxious when he leaves? Is the facility clean? Do they require vaccinations and flea-control products? If you prefer a different look, ask the groomer if she has more than one option for the style. Use your instincts and change groomers if you or your pet don't feel comfortable.

During COVID, most groomers are allowing only curbside service. It may take a long time to revert back to allowing you to accompany your dog inside.

Most professional groomers can groom any breed. If you have a particular "look" in mind, take a photo to the groomers so they know what your expectations are. If they don't get it right the first time, don't worry. The difference between a good haircut and a bad one is ... two weeks. Give them another chance if your puppy came home happy.

If you choose to do your own coat care, you will need shampoo, appropriate combs and/or brushes, and a high-speed dog dryer. A human hair dryer will take you all weekend to achieve a dry coat. In some locations, there are self-serve dog washes at dog facilities and some car washes.

Nail Care

Nail trims scare most owners, mostly because they seem to upset most dogs. Owners know if they trim a nail too short, the dog will be uncomfortable, and it will be messy when your puppy tracks blood through the house. But untrimmed nails lead to foot pain and the likelihood of a torn nail, which will be even messier than a nail trim gone wrong.

Start with weekly trimming of the tips of your puppy's sharp little nails with an appropriate nail trimmer. Use peanut butter or another slow-eating treat to keep the puppy distracted. Having two people trim nails helps a lot: one to feed and hold, and the other to trim. At first, just do one or two nails – you don't need to do all 18 (16 if there are no dewclaws and 20 if there are front and rear dewclaws) in one sitting. As your puppy matures, and you get better at trimming nails, you can eventually do all the nails at once. Starting young and doing little bits frequently will help your puppy learn to accept this procedure and make her life easier.

Many dogs still have their dewclaws. All dogs are born with front dewclaws; some dogs are born with single or double rear dewclaws. While these are normal, the rear ones in particular can become problematic. They may be covered with long hair and are often overlooked when the nails are being trimmed. Be sure to trim them so your dog won't have them grow around like a ram's horn and dig into the skin on the inside of the leg. This can be painful for the dog, and can cause lameness.

An alternative to a nail clipper is using a Dremel or other rotary tool with a grinding wheel. Again, have two people, lots of peanut butter and just do one or two nails. Anchor your hand by placing your thumb firmly on the puppy's foot and keep the rest of your hand wrapped securely around the rotary tool to keep it from bouncing around.

Your third choice is to teach your dog to use a nail board – a board wrapped with sandpaper that your dog scratches with his front feet to wear down his nails. Of course, the back feet will still need nail care, but those nails tend to be shorter than the front nails.

Your final choice is to bail completely and pay your groomer or veterinarian to trim your dog's nails.

Equipment to have on hand is a Dremel with a grinding wheel or a sharpened nail trimmer. Also, have either styptic powder, a dry bar of soap or flour to put on the nail if you zig, then zag, and end up with a nail that's too short and bleeding. You can slide a sock over your puppy's foot to protect it if you have an accident with the nail clipper.

Ear Care

All puppies should become accustomed to having their ears handled by you and your veterinary professionals. Just like touching feet and brushing teeth, handling is a great way to have your puppy accept ear care if it becomes necessary.

However, if it ain't broke, don't fix it. Many dogs go through life without ever having an ear infection. Ear infections are most common in dogs with flop ears (as opposed to upright ears), dogs that need grooming (which means they grow hair in their ears while breeds that don't need grooming have hairless ear canals) and dogs with allergies. Teaching your dog to have her ears touched is a great idea. Putting ear-cleaning solutions in her ears without a reason is not a good idea.

If you have a dog with hairy ears that lead to an ear infection, talk to your veterinary professional about using Nair™ (yes, the stuff women use on their legs to eliminate hair), which is safe to use in dog's ears. The one with aloe is most soothing. Apply the Nair™ carefully so a head shake from the puppy doesn't lead to a blob on your face, wiping out an eyebrow or two.

Ask your veterinary professional about ear cleaning. Products with alcohol, peroxide and other solutions can foam or sting, and be painful. Only use veterinary-approved products, not do-it-yourself ear products, as these could cause damage to your dog's ear canals and eardrums.

CHAPTER 10

Veterinary Care

Great veterinary care can be expensive. However, if you are loyal to your veterinary professionals, and get to know them well, you will be able to provide great care for your new puppy. Let the veterinary-care team know what your preferences are before the appointment so they can help meet your needs.

Everyone on the veterinary team should make you feel comfortable, starting with the receptionist who schedules your appointment. Your experience in the lobby, how your pet is managed in the exam room to keep anxiety levels as low as possible, the way the doctor explains exam findings and administers treatments – everything should put you at ease. Will the visit be perfect, and will you and your dog never feel stressed? No, of course not. But trust your instincts: If you think the veterinary team could do a better job, either share your wishes with them or change veterinary clinics.

How do I select a veterinarian?

Many clients travel a long distance for veterinary care. The closest veterinarian to your home, while handy, may not be your best choice.

The right veterinarian for you and your family should ...

... provide the services you feel are important. If you are a new puppy owner, you may not know what you want or need. The more experienced you are in dog ownership, the more you know what you want. Ask about services you find important, as veterinarians may not list all of them on their website.

... agree with you philosophically on your puppy's care. Will this vet work with you to determine the frequency of vaccinations, based on your pet's lifestyle and your opinions on vaccines? The age to spay or neuter is a life-changing decision – will this vet support you in delaying this procedure? If you have a purebred or purpose-bred dog, or a rescue or foster dog, is the vet supportive of this choice? If you plan to breed your dog, will he be critical of this decision or support you in this role? If you prefer to be present for all out-patient procedures, will your vet allow this? During the pandemic, you and your family may be confined to your car for curbside service. But you can ask how the veterinary clinic usually handles these requests. Is the veterinary team supportive of keeping your pet emotionally and physically comfortable while they provide care?

... have hours that are convenient for your work schedule. How does the veterinarian handle after-hour emergencies? Does the clinic have a system to help triage the urgency of cases?

You should feel comfortable "interviewing" your prospective veterinarian, even if it must be done virtually, by phone or video conference. You may even ask for a tour of the hospital when there is an opportunity to show you around. This can be done virtually. Dr. Nancy Kay wrote a fantastic book called "Your Dog's Best Health: A Dozen Reasonable Things to Expect From Your Vet" that I strongly recommend you read and take to heart.

You must be your pet's health-care advocate – make certain you trust and love your veterinarian and her team. People who choose a veterinary career are caring and hard working. They are there to help you provide great care. Ask them for help with any pet-related needs.

Veterinary Exams

You *can* teach your dog to cooperate with veterinary professionals *if* you practice and *if* you go to a veterinary facility that is open to cooperative veterinary care.

Dr. Karen Overall has YouTube videos that demonstrate the skills you can teach your dog regarding cooperation. You can teach dogs to allow blood to be drawn, catheters to be placed, even to hold their breath while an X-ray is being taken. That last video is 13 minutes long, so grab a drink, sit back and learn! It's very cool.

Be certain you are working with a veterinary team that is willing to go the extra mile to make you and your dog comfortable. Veterinary clinics can participate in Fear Free, Cooperative Care and Low Stress Handling® methods. Even without this certification, most veterinary team members are kind, caring, compassionate, patient people who want the best for your dog.

In general, as a caregiver, you should be allowed to be a participant in most of your dog's care. Many dogs are calmer with their "person" present. Of course, for safety reasons, you cannot be in the surgery room (to maintain a sterile environment) or the X-ray room (because of exposure to X-ray beams).

During the pandemic, many veterinary clinics are requiring pet owners to wait in their cars. After COVID-19 settles down, if you are not allowed to see what your pet is having done, perhaps you need to ask about it or seek an alternate care facility.

That being said, some dogs are calmer without their owner present. Some dogs think they need to protect you from the veterinary staff – of course, they don't really understand we are not there to harm either of you. When you are holding your dog, and a veterinary team member attempts to pick up and place your dog on the exam table, the dog may try to protect you. I prefer the caregiver leave the room, rather than the pet being removed. This allows the pet to remain in the space to which he's already acclimated. Once care is completed, the owner returns.

Another way you can make veterinary visits better for your dog is to go when nothing "bad" is going to happen. This means the dog comes in, goes into the exam room, on and off the exam table, hangs out and eats some treats, catches a ball, and leaves. No injections, no thermometer, no exam – just good times. Send along your own treats – your veterinary clinic can't have all of your dog's favorite snacks in stock. I use lots of spray cheese, peanut butter (if not allergic), gingersnaps, chicken baby food and cheese puffs.

Again, if your veterinary clinic is limiting visits during the pandemic, this too will have to wait. Try to find a veterinary team that is willing to work with you and your dog on this. Of course, you should always call first or make an appointment to avoid the busiest part of the day, so staff has the time to work with you on this important aspect of your dog's care.

Core Vaccines

These are the vaccinations that are recommended by all the thought leaders in veterinary medicine. Plan on having your puppy receive these vaccinations in an appropriate series.

DAPPv = Distemper, adenovirus, parainfluenza and parvovirus. All four components protect against viral infections, none of which have been eradicated from dogs in the United States. Distemper can cause life-threatening respiratory, neurological and intestinal disease; adenovirus affects the liver; parainfluenza can cause respiratory disease, and parvovirus can cause life-threatening vomiting and diarrhea.

This vaccination, DAPPv, is typically given at six to eight weeks for the first vaccination, 12 weeks for the second vaccination, and 16 to 18 weeks for the third. Sometimes, more vaccines are administered, based on the lifestyle, breeder and age the series is initiated.

Some veterinary clinics consistently map the location of the injection site, in case a lump develops.

Once the DAPPv series is completed, this vaccination is boostered at 15 months for most dogs' lifestyles, then usually every three years thereafter.

Some veterinary clinics are still recommending annual vaccinations after 15 months of age, even though most dogs have longer immunity than one year. Finding a veterinary clinic that is progressive, uses high-quality vaccines that confer longer-lasting immunity, and does not vaccinate for all diseases annually can actually save you money – not to mention your dog's life.

Leptospirosis (Lepto). This vaccination usually includes four strains of leptospirosis. It may be combined with DAPPv, allowing for just one immunization. Leptospirosis is a bacterial infection that can lead to liver and kidney disease as well as pneumonia. It can be serious enough to cause the death of a patient.

Lepto is spread through the urine of infected wild and domestic animals like cattle and mice, in water sources, and can also be shared with humans. Standing water or dewy grass in your yard or even a city street can expose your dog. Typically, the first lepto vaccination is administered at 12 weeks of age, then again three to four weeks later. Thereafter, this should be boostered every year, based on lifestyle and the region of the country in which the dog resides.

Rabies. This is the only immunization required by law for all dogs and, in some municipalities, cats. Because rabies is a fatal disease and contagious to humans, we take this vaccination seriously. The first rabies vaccination can be given at three to five months of age and is valid for one year, with the subsequent vaccination typically valid for three years. This vaccination *must* be administered by a veterinarian or a certified veterinary technician under the direct supervision of a veterinarian. A certificate signed by the veterinary professional and tag are provided as proof of vaccination.

Non-Core Vaccines

Non-core vaccines are not considered mandatory, but may be recommended based on your dog's lifestyle.

Bordetella/Parainfluenza/Adenovirus. This grouping of bacterial and viral diseases causes upper respiratory disease. It is also known as kennel cough or canine infectious respiratory disease (CIRD). It is easily spread dog to dog by shared water bowls, coughing, barking and sneezing in a crowded environment such as a dog-grooming or boarding facility or a dog park. The three-way vaccine can be administered by nose drops. The oral vaccine protects against bordetella and adenovirus but does not protect against parainfluenza. The injectable vaccine is not as effective as the intranasal vaccine. Rarely, bordetella can infect immunocompromised people.

Canine Influenza (bivalent). Canine influenza, similar to influenza in other species, causes respiratory disease. It is one cause of pneumonia, sometimes hemorrhagic, and can be fatal. There are two recently mutated strains of the canine influenza virus – H3N2 and H3N8. Because they are novel, or new viruses, no dogs have natural immunity. The first year, two immunizations are administered three to four weeks apart, with an annual booster thereafter.

If your dog co-mingles with other dogs at the dog park, groomer, day care, training classes or with friends' and family's dogs, discuss this vaccination with your veterinarian. In general, if bordetella is recommended based on your dog's lifestyle, the bivalent canine-influenza vaccination probably should be, too.

Canine Coronavirus.
There are two strains of canine coronavirus: one that causes vomiting and diarrhea, and one that causes upper respiratory disease. There is no indication that the current COVID-19 human strain can cause disease in dogs or that the canine form can cause disease in humans. Both the enteric (vomiting and diarrhea) and respiratory strains tend to be mild in dogs over six weeks of age. As a result, most dogs are not vaccinated for the enteric strain. There is no vaccine for the respiratory strain.

Lyme disease.
Lyme (not Lyme's) disease is caused by a spirochete bacteria and most commonly causes fever, malaise and lameness. However, it has been associated with other disorders, some serious, like Lyme nephritis, which can cause kidney failure and death.

Lyme disease is most commonly transmitted to dogs via the bite of a deer tick, although

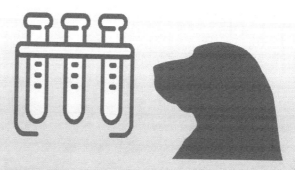

TITERS

A titer (pronounced TYE-ter) is a blood test that will assess your puppy's response to the distemper and parvovirus vaccines. Up to 10 percent of dogs fail to mount an adequate antibody response to vaccines. If your dog has protective antibodies, he may not need an annual or triannual booster. Distemper and parvovirus are the only two viral diseases we can routinely titer-test for in dogs. (The titer test for leptospirosis is to assess disease exposure, not antibody development.)

As we have seen a movement away from routine annual vaccinations, we have seen titer testing increase in popularity and demand. You may want to ask your veterinary professional to order this blood test instead of routinely boostering your dog for distemper and parvovirus annually.

Titers can reduce the frequency of vaccination administration. There is some concern that certain dogs will have unfortunate vaccine reactions, making less frequent vaccinations safer.

MICROCHIPS

A microchip is a small device placed under the skin of your dog that is passively present until activated by the wand or scanner, displaying your pet's unique microchip number on the device. The microchip is not a tracking device, and no personal information is available on it. Although the insertion with a needle over the shoulders is quick and nearly painless, many elect to have this done during their dog's spay or neuter.

Microchip are very affordable, and are a definitive way to prove your dog is indeed yours. One in three dogs goes missing in his lifetime. So if the unthinkable happens and your dog disappears, a working microchip will significantly improve the chances you and your pet will be reunited.

other vectors are likely involved as well. It is seen in all 50 states but is most common in New England and the upper Midwest. Even dogs that do not live in these regions but that run in wooded areas or fields of tall grass are at risk of picking up ticks that can transmit the bacteria.

Lyme disease is the only tick-borne disease for which we can vaccinate dogs. The first year, the dog receives two vaccinations, two to three weeks apart, with an annual booster. However, the vaccine should not be relied on as the sole protection for our dogs. Counterintuitively, the deer tick is most active from December to March. So use appropriate tick-control products to keep ticks off your dog and out of your personal environment as well.

This disease, as well as anaplasmosis and ehrlichia, also tick-borne, are frequently tested for when we test for heartworm disease. (See the next chapter.)

Dental Care

Dental care isn't just about bad breath. It is about the overall health of your dog. Advanced dental disease leads to heart, kidney and other disorders.

While dental chews, special dental diets and water additives can help reduce dental disease, nothing can replace brushing. Your dentist doesn't tell you chewing gum or eating cheese is a substitute for brushing and flossing your teeth. The same is true for your dog. (Don't worry – we don't expect you to floss!)

Starting your puppy young with good dental hygiene is critical for keeping his mouth and body healthy. Brushing your puppy's teeth is the single best way to keep your dog off your veterinarian's dental cleaning table, undergoing dental care with full general anesthesia. When you start young, your puppy will be more accepting of the handling required, the feel of the toothbrush, and the taste of the doggie toothpaste. Getting into a routine so you are doing this at the same time every day means your dog will become accustomed to the process. Offering an appropriate treat such as cheese (good for dental health) after the brushing session will help your new puppy look forward to this time you spend together.

The good news is you don't have to open your dog's mouth to brush his teeth. Dogs don't have flat molars like we do; because they are pointed, they don't accumulate food. Just slide the toothbrush along the parts of the teeth that touch the lips, and brush.

You already know what that feels like from brushing your own or your children's teeth. Placing your dog on an elevated surface such as the top of your washing machine with a non-slip mat will help him sit still.

Find a small, soft toothbrush and a flavor of toothpaste (beef, poultry, malt) you think your dog will appreciate and start brushing! Avoid using human toothpaste, as the taste is unappealing and the sudsing effect may cause an upset stomach if swallowed.

Teething

Teething is not always related to chewing. Unfortunately, many dogs happily chew inappropriate objects before and long after they are done teething.

Puppies start teething at four months of age, beginning with the incisors, the six small upper and lower teeth in front. Teething progresses back to the premolars and molars. By five to five and half months, the four canine teeth, or fang teeth, have erupted. Some puppies, especially small breeds, may have baby teeth that are not replaced by their adult teeth and end up with both sets, looking like a shark. If you suspect this has happened, have your veterinary professional take a look – you don't want the extra teeth to remain, as this can lead to malalignment of the teeth as well as premature development of tartar.

Spaying and Neutering

Since the 1970s, dogs in the U.S. have routinely been spayed or neutered. The social impact and importance of spaying and neutering over the last 50 years to minimize dog overpopulation cannot be overstated.

However, at this time, there is not a dog overpopulation concern in most of the U.S. In fact, due to pet acquisition changes during the COVID-19 pandemic, there is an apparent dog shortage in most states.

Historically, dogs and cats have been spayed or neutered at six months of age or, recently, even younger. The pet-owning public and veterinary community have long believed this will lead to healthier, longer-lived dogs. But there is mounting scientific evidence that this is not the case.

While there are health benefits to spaying and neutering, they must be weighed against the health benefits of retaining the sex hormones by leaving your pet intact. The primary disadvantage of delaying or not altering your pet is that hormones can lead to unwanted sexual behaviors and unwanted pregnancies. Not spaying also leaves females at risk of pyometra (uterine infection) and mammary tumors.

Advantages of *not* spaying or neutering include:

- Reduced risk of obesity in males and females.

- Reduced risk of hip dysplasia, torn cruciate (ACL) ligaments and other orthopedic disorders. Waiting to spay or neuter your dog will allow the growth plates to close at a more appropriate time, leading to dogs who are slightly shorter in status and with better joint angulation. Fewer orthopedic problems may also be related to reduced risk of obesity.

- Reduced risk of prostate cancer (prostatic adenocarcinoma) in males. This is in direct conflict with what you may have been told in the past.

- Reduced risk of bone cancer (osteosarcoma), lymph-node cancer (lymphoma), bladder cancer (transitional cell carcinoma) and spleen cancer (hemangiosarcoma).

- Reduced risk of allergies.

- Reduced risk of low-thyroid disease (hypothyroidism).

- Reduced risk of urinary leaking (incontinence) and bladder infections, primarily in females.

- Reduced incidence of adverse reactions to vaccines.

- Less aggression toward people and animals in females.

- Reduced incidence of senility (canine cognitive dysfunction).

- Less fearfulness and noise phobias.

In general, the larger the dog, the greater the benefits of delaying or avoiding removing the ovaries or testes.

If your puppy has already been spayed or neutered, there is nothing you can do to change his or her hormonal status. At this time, hormone-replacement therapy is not a mainstream treatment for dogs. Also, be aware this dog needs to eat 25 percent fewer calories to avoid obesity.

Other Options

One alternative is to do an ovary-sparing spay (removing the uterus but not the ovaries) or a vasectomy. Your female will still have heat cycles, and your male will still have sexual behaviors, but with retained ovaries or testes, your dog is likely to have a longer, healthier life, and can't reproduce.

Based on the research available, it is clear there are a number of health benefits of retaining the sex steroid hormones. This benefit varies with age, sex and breed. Although surgically altering your dog to be unable to breed may be the responsible choice for many dogs, it is in the best interest of each individual patient for a veterinarian to assess the risks and benefits of gonadectomy (removing the testes or ovaries versus vasectomy or ovary-sparing spay). Discuss this decision and have your veterinarian advise you on what is appropriate for each individual dog at each stage of its life.

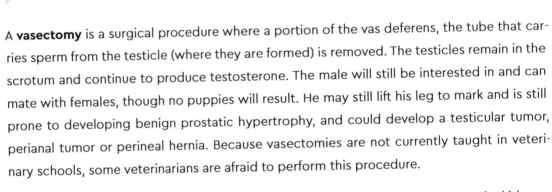

What is a vasectomy? What is an ovary-sparing spay?

A **vasectomy** is a surgical procedure where a portion of the vas deferens, the tube that carries sperm from the testicle (where they are formed) is removed. The testicles remain in the scrotum and continue to produce testosterone. The male will still be interested in and can mate with females, though no puppies will result. He may still lift his leg to mark and is still prone to developing benign prostatic hypertrophy, and could develop a testicular tumor, perianal tumor or perineal hernia. Because vasectomies are not currently taught in veterinary schools, some veterinarians are afraid to perform this procedure.

An ovary-sparing spay is when one or both ovaries are left in the abdomen, near the kidneys, but the uterus and cervix are removed. Because the uterus is removed, the female will not be able to become pregnant, even if a mating occurs. The female will still have heat cycles and be attractive to male dogs. She will have little to no bloody vaginal discharge during her heat cycles. Because the uterus is removed down to and including the cervix, she cannot develop a pyometra. This is not well understood by many veterinarians who have not been trained in this. As a result, many veterinarians are unwilling to perform this new procedure. As with vasectomy, ovary-sparing spays are not part of veterinary-school curriculum, leaving some veterinarians leery about the procedure and concerned about legal ramifications because of lack of comprehension of benefits and risks.

What are the disadvantages of retaining the testes or ovaries?

- Increased risk of mammary (breast) cancer in intact females. This risk of breast cancer increases with each subsequent cycle and the benefit of spaying does not disappear until the animal reaches old age. Mammary cancer is one of the most common types of cancer in small animals, and is malignant less than 50 percent of the time in dogs. Very few dogs die from breast cancer due to low metastatic rates and early detection and treatment.

- Increased risk of ovarian cancer in intact females, though incidence and mortality risk are very low.

- Increased risk of testicular cancer in intact males. The incidence for testicular cancer is common, but malignancy and mortality are very low.

- An increased risk of pyometra in intact female dogs, which increases with age. (Varies by breed – review with your vet.)

- Risk of unwanted pregnancies if an ovarian-sparing spay or vasectomy is not performed.

- Increased risk of prostatitis, benign prostatic hyperplasia, prostatic cysts and squamous metaplasia of the prostate in males. Neutering at a later age will resolve these disorders.

- Increased incidence of perineal and inguinal hernia and perineal adenoma in intact males.

- Inter-dog aggression, which may be due to competition for available territory or availability of cycling animals.

- Increased risk of wandering and being hit by a car in intact dogs.

- Increased incidence of urinary marking in intact males.

- Ongoing sexual behaviors, including heat cycles in females with an ovary-sparing spay.

If you choose surgery, at what age should you "alter" your pet?

If you opt for a non-traditional vasectomy or ovary-sparing spay, you may do this at any age, and as young as eight weeks. Because the sex organs are left to function, your dog will still have his or her hormones.

By contrast, with traditional neuter or spay, age is important. Since gonadectomy prior to puberty or sexual maturity may make the risks of some diseases higher in certain breeds or individuals, the option to leave your pet intact should be available to you.

Many times, I recommend waiting until at least six months of age, or older, usually past puberty, to allow skeletal maturity, due to health and behavioral advantages. For canine athletes, Dr. Christine Zink recommends **waiting until after 14 months of age (the age at which the growth plates have closed) for males and females to be neutered or spayed.**

The age at which you spay or neuter may be the biggest decision you make regarding your dog's health, as it affects longevity, health and quality of life. Discuss this with your veterinary professional before you schedule your puppy or dog for this life-altering procedure.

CHAPTER 11

Parasite Control

Our furry little family members all too often bring parasites into our environment. Fortunately, most of these are not shared with us. However, we need to be vigilant and use appropriate parasite-control products for the safety and health of our dogs, and ourselves.

Internal Parasites

Roundworms

There are two kinds of roundworms (ascarids) commonly seen in our dogs – *Toxocara* and *Toxascaris*. There is no real value in distinguishing between the two.

Adult roundworms may be seen in the stools of infected dogs, and look like long pieces of spaghetti with pointed ends. However, not seeing the roundworms does not ensure that your puppy is parasite free.

Most puppies are born with or are infected with roundworms shortly after birth, unless the mother dog was on a very specific (and not commonly used) parasite-control program during pregnancy. Roundworms can migrate to the puppies through the placenta. Older puppies and adults are exposed by directly ingesting the parasite eggs from the environment as well as other vertebrate hosts such as rabbits and mice that have baby roundworms in their tissues.

FECAL EXAMS AND STOOL SAMPLES

Fecal exams and stool samples are the same thing: Your vet takes a sample of feces from your dog, mix it with special solutions, and examine it in one of three ways. Most common is a fecal flotation test, in which the sample is centrifuged and the part of the fluid at the top of the tube is examined microscopically, which will usually show the eggs of the parasite(s) in question. The second, a more sensitive test called an ELISA test, is also done with feces, but is evaluated based on finding the protein of the parasite. The least sensitive method is to look at the feces in a direct smear under the microscope.

Ideally, puppies should be tested several times during their vaccination series. The Centers for Disease Control (CDC) and the Companion Animal Parasite Council (www.CAPCvet.org) recommend that adult dogs be tested twice yearly, to protect them and their human family against intestinal parasites.

The fecal flotation test is effective in finding roundworm, hookworm and whipworm eggs as well as coccidia. The ELISA test is more sensitive in diagnosing roundworms, hookworms, whipworms and giardia. At this time, there is no ELISA test for tapeworms and coccidia. Most tapeworm infestations are detected by visual observation of the tapeworm segments on the rectum of the dog or fresh feces. This can be upsetting to owners who have observed tapeworm segments but receive a "no parasite seen" fecal analysis report. If this is the case with your dog, report your findings to your vet.

Adult roundworms live by freely floating in a dog's intestines. Puppies may have no symptoms, have diarrhea and/or vomiting, have a pot-bellied, unthrifty appearance, poor coat, and be unable to grow and gain weight.

Young puppies can be so severely infected with roundworms that they become sick or die. They can also be infected with a heavy parasite load before the stool sample shows a positive result. For these reasons, as well as the fact that humans can become infected and sick from roundworms, too, it is recommended that puppies are dewormed every two weeks starting at two weeks of age and continuing until at least eight weeks. At that point, oral heartworm preventives containing roundworm treatment can be started. Frequent deworming and fecal testing are essential for protecting both puppies and humans in the household.

There are several good deworming medications on the market, some of which are not prescription items. All are effective, but accurate weighing of the puppy and dosing of medication are necessary. In addition to medication, using a detergent product to scrupulously clean and remove fecal material is essential.

Medications most commonly used for roundworm control are pyrantel pamoate, piperazine, fenbendazole, milbemycin and moxidectin (alone or in combination with heartworm medications).

Roundworms are the most common zoonotic parasitic infection – that is, an infection a human gets from a dog. Children, the elderly and people with immunosuppressive conditions are most commonly affected. Because the roundworms do not just stay in the intestines but migrate through the body, the liver, lungs and eyes can be permanently damaged. Good personal hygiene and meticulous parasite control are essential in protecting people from this common dog parasite.

Hookworms

Hookworms come in three forms: *Ancylostoma caninum*, *Ancylostoma brazilense* and *Uncinaria stenocephala*. As with roundworms, the species is not of clinical significance, and many puppies are born infected soon after birth: The larval worms go through the mammary glands, swallowed with the milk. Puppies and dogs can also become infected by ingesting larvae in the environment, larval penetration through their skin, ingesting other vertebrate hosts with infected larvae, or by eating cockroaches that contain infective larvae.

Unlike roundworms, hookworms are rarely detected by looking at the feces.

Hookworms can cause more serious symptoms than roundworms. They attach to the lining of the intestines, digest the tissues, inject an anticoagulant into the tissues, and suck blood through the intestinal wall. They may live from four to 24 months in the intestines. This aggressive feeding can lead to puppies who become anemic, fail to grow and gain weight, look unthrifty, have a poor coat, become dehydrated, and have dark, tarry, loose stools. With a severe enough infection, puppies can die. Puppies may also have symptoms of pneumonia. Rarely, skin lesions can be associated with hookworm migration in dogs.

Because puppies can also be infected before stool samples come up positive, and because they can infect humans, deworming should start at two weeks of age and continue every two weeks until at least eight weeks of age. The mother dog should be dewormed on the same days as the pups. At eight weeks, oral heartworm preventives containing hookworm treatment can be started. Frequent deworming and fecal testing are essential.

There are several good non-prescription deworming medications on the market; be sure to weigh the puppy carefully to calculate the correct dose. As with roundworm, clean up feces and wash all bedding.

Medications most commonly used for hookworm control are pyrantel pamoate, fenbendazole, milbemycin and moxidectin (alone or in combination with heartworm medications).

Humans can become infected with hookworms via direct skin penetration with the infective larva. This is most common in warmer high-humidity climates. Rarely, hookworms can migrate through the intestines of a human. Keeping feces picked up, and wearing shoes and gloves in potentially infected environments will help protect against this zoonotic disease.

Whipworms

This parasite comes in one form – *Trichuris vulpis* – and can be seen with the naked eye, though it is rarely reported by owners.

Whipworms are transmitted to dogs only by ingesting eggs containing infective larvae from the environment. It is not transmitted from the mother or from ingesting infected animals. The eggs, although visible on fecal examinations, are shed intermittently, hiding in the cecum, leading to undetected infestations.

Whipworms may cause no symptoms in dogs. They may cause intermittent diarrhea but rarely lead to serious infestations. There are few reports of zoonotic infections.

Medications used to treat whipworms include fenbendazole, a combination of febantel, pyrantel pamoate and praziquantel, or milbemycin (alone or in a heartworm-preventive combination product). These need to be repeated once a month for three consecutive months or longer to achieve control.

Tapeworms

There are several species of tapeworms, including multiple species of *Taenia*, *Diphyllobothrium* and *Echinococcus*.

The most common way of diagnosing tapeworms is by observing tapeworm segments on the rectum/underside of your dog's tail or on the fresh feces from your dog (or on your pillowcase). They rarely show up on fecal samples.

Taenia tapeworms are spread to dogs when they eat an infected animal, including rodents, pigs, sheep, rabbits, deer or horses. The tapeworm uses the hooks of its mouth to attach to the lining of the dog's intestines. *Diphyllobothrium* tapeworms are spread when dogs ingest infected fish, including perch, pike and walleye. *Echinococcus* has sheep and rodents as the intermediate host.

Most tapeworms cause no or mild symptoms in infected dogs. If symptoms are present, they include diarrhea, weight loss and vomiting.

Praziquantel, alone or in combination with heartworm preventive, will treat *Taenia* and *Echinococcus* infections. Fenbendazole will treat *Taenia pisiformis*. Preventing ingestion of rabbits, rodents, fish and other vertebrates will prevent reinfection. No treatment has been approved for *Diphyllobothrium*.

Taenia and *Diphyllobothrium* are not commonly spread from dogs to humans. *Echinococcus* can infect humans, causing serious disease, including hydatid cysts.

Giardia

Giardia is a one-celled, flagellated parasite frequently seen in all dogs, though it is more likely to cause diarrhea in young rather than older dogs. It is common among dogs raised in groups such as shelters, rescues and breeder facilities, and can be associated with contaminated water sources. The reported incidence of 15 percent may be understated in larger groups. Although giardia does not cause serious disease, the associated diarrhea makes crate training and housebreaking more difficult. It frequently recurs after treatment.

Metronidazole, fenbendazole and febantel are the prescription drugs used most commonly to manage giardia. These medications may need to be used together to control the symptoms. Other medications are sometimes used, but are not approved in dogs for use by the FDA. Additionally, intestinal diets and probiotics can be helpful in controlling symptoms.

Giardia is diagnosed by either a microscopic fecal examination or by an ELISA test, which detects the parasite's antigen. The ELISA test may remain positive for an extended period of time, even after treatment has been successful. Giardia seems to rarely be transmitted from dogs to humans. Good hygiene such as hand-washing and picking up stools is important to reduce spread. The cysts can be difficult to eliminate from the environment, with quaternary ammonium disinfectants appearing to be most effective.

Coccidia

Coccidia is a single-celled protozoan parasite. There are two varieties, *Isospora* and *Eimeria*. As with other parasites, there is no real value in distinguishing between them. What has value is a laboratory technician who can distinguish between a dog parasite and one from another species that is just "passing through" from something the puppy ate. When the coccidia is identified as a non-dog parasite, treatment is not warranted.

Coccidia, like giardia, are frequently seen in puppies coming from breeders, shelters and rescue organizations alike. They are nearly ubiquitous in young puppies and dogs. The good news is although they cause diarrhea, they rarely cause serious disease. It is annoying more than serious.

Most medications are coccidiostatic (not coccidiocidal), meaning the medications on the market approved for dogs will slow down but won't kill coccidia.

There are some medications used by breeders and rescues that are not FDA approved for use in dogs. Instead, I recommend sticking with Albon, an approved drug.

One innovative way to both manage coccidia and reduce the risk of picking up parvovirus during transport is to use Albon the last three days at the rescue or breeder and the first three days at the puppy's new home. This protocol stabilizes the normal bacteria in the puppy's GI tract, reducing the risk of parvovirus setting up housekeeping in your puppy. This is *not* an admission that a sick puppy is being transferred to you, but rather the sign of a conscientious party who wants you to have a happy, healthy new puppy in your home.

Heartworm

Heartworm disease is almost exactly what it sounds like – worms that live in the heart and lungs of our dogs. This life-threatening disease is spread by the bite of a mosquito that recently bit a heartworm-infected dog or wild canine. These worms are six to 12 inches long and can live in your dog for up to two years.

How can a mosquito transmit a 12-inch worm? The adult heartworms produce baby heartworms called microfilaria. They are microscopic, about the width of one red blood cell. These microfilaria circulate in the infected dog's bloodstream. The mosquito that bites a heartworm-positive dog ingests the microfilaria, the microfilaria molt inside the mosquito, become infectious, and are transmitted into another dog with the next mosquito bite. Even dogs who spend most of their time indoors get bitten by mosquitoes, making all dogs susceptible to this infection.

Heartworm is easily preventable by using a monthly chewable treat containing ivermectin or milbemycin. Most heartworm preventives also include a variety of medications that control intestinal parasites, including pyrantel and/or praziquantel. There is also an effective and safe injection that lasts 12 months that contains moxidectin. The recommendation is to use year-round heartworm preventive, even in northern climates, as these medications also control the most common intestinal parasites.

External Parasites

Fleas

Fleas are nasty little parasitic insects that will happily bite and take blood meals from your dogs, cats, other mammals and, yes, even you and your family. Fleas are reddish-brown, shiny, six-legged, tiny, wingless, flat (side-to-side), high-jumping parasites that spend nearly their whole adult lives on the dog.

In various stages of their lifecycle, they can survive for more than 100 days in the home or other environment. Female fleas bite dogs, and lay eggs that drop off the dog. The eggs hatch into larvae, which molt over nine to 200 days, spin a cocoon, and can stay in the environment for up to one year before a new flea emerges to catch a ride on the next dog that goes past. The pupae in the cocoon will emerge as new fleas when they sense movement, vibrations, heat and carbon dioxide, all indicating the presence of an eligible new host – aka your dog or you! Warm weather and high humidity encourage flea development.

In general, dogs get fleas from being in a contaminated environment, not from an infected dog or other mammal. Unfortunately, the larval cocoon is resistant to most insecticides, drying, freezing temperatures and the IGRs (insect growth regulators) we have available for flea control.

How do you know if your dog has fleas? Flea bites can make your dog itchy and develop a rash, particularly if she has an allergy to fleas. Many other skin conditions can cause rashes and scratching. Spotting even one adult flea is a diagnosis. However, fleas move fast and are hard to see, particularly if you have a dog with a dark-colored coat. Finding flea dirt (known as frass, which is flea feces) is strongly suggestive of a flea infestation. Flea dirt is a dark-brown, comma-shaped granular material that exudes a rust-colored ring when placed on a wet paper towel. Real dirt does not do the same thing. In severe cases, usually in puppies, the fleas can take so much blood they cause anemia.

Many dogs that are not allergic to fleas can harbor a large population of fleas without any symptoms of scratching or hair loss. Yuk! Use preventive year-round to keep this from happening to you and your dog.

Ticks

Ticks are the other nasty, common, feared parasite we frequently find on our dogs. Unfortunately, we can find them on ourselves, too – either from our dogs bringing them into our environment or from us sharing the same outdoor space with our dogs.

THREE OPTIONS FOR PREVENTION

Generally, there are three categories of medications that both prevent and treat fleas and ticks: topicals (tubes of liquid applied to a dog's back and shoulders), orals (chewable pills) and collars. The new versions of tick collars are far more effective than what we used in the past.

Some of the topical preventives also prevent the critters from staying on the dog long enough to bite. The orals have the advantage of being neater and less oily than the topicals. If you have children in the home, this may make you feel safer about using flea or tick preventives. Orals have no repellent effect against any flying or biting insects such as mosquitoes and flies. There are limited reports of a small subset of dogs who develop tremors and seizures associated with all of the oral medications in this drug class (isooxazolines). These products should not be used in seizure-prone dogs. Duration of activity varies from four weeks to 12 weeks.

Some flea and tick medications are by prescription only; others are available over the counter. Counterintuitively, some prescription products are safer than those available through non-prescription sources. Products come to market frequently and are often game changers.

See the Flea and Tick Primer and the Flea/Tick/Heartworm charts at the end of this chapter for a summary of choices.

Like fleas, the female tick requires a blood meal to reproduce. Unlike fleas, the adult female tick attaches with her mouth parts, biting and staying attached to the host (you, your dog or other wildlife) for several days while feeding, then drops off to lay her eggs. The male tick is often found attached beneath her, but does not engorge with a blood meal.

If you find a tick attached to you or your dog, remove her carefully, wearing gloves to prevent transmission to you. Avoid squeezing her body during removal, as this will inject diseases into you or your dog. Using a tick key, tick twister or tweezers, grasp the tick close to the skin and pull straight out. You will not leave the head of the tick behind. After removing the engorged female tick, go back to that site, look again, and if present, remove her male partner. Avoid using other techniques such as a match or Vaseline. If there are larger numbers than you can remove, seek veterinary care for tick-control products as soon as possible.

There are many species of ticks. Most of the clinically significant ones in the United States are hard ticks. There are differences in where they live geographically across North America. Because ticks are active throughout the year in most geographical areas, and because of the diseases they transmit to our dogs and us, tick-control products should be used year round, not only for the health of our pets but to keep ticks from invading our environment and spreading disease to us as well.

Ticks find us and our dogs when we are walking through leaf litter, tall grass and the understory of trees. If ticks are found in large numbers, you can modify the habitat around your home or property to make it harder for ticks and wildlife hosts like deer and mice that support them. This includes keeping the grass cut short, removing leaf litter and brush, minimizing ground-cover plants, and selecting plants that do not attract deer. These areas can be treated with carbaryl, cyfluthrin, permethrin or s-fenvalerate to help control tick pressure. Outdoor tick management advice can be found at www.cdc.gov/ticks/avoid/in_the_yard.html.

If you or your pet have a tick, remove it, place it in rubbing alcohol, and save it in the freezer if needed later for identification, should you or your pet become ill.

With climate change, we are seeing shifts in tick populations and the geographical areas they inhabit. Tick distributions are dynamic and ever changing. New medications approved by the FDA and EPA are coming to market. Stay attentive to the new products and the diseases and ticks in your region.

Why should we worry about ticks?

Not only are ticks unappealing parasites that attach to us and our dogs; they can carry diseases that can make our dogs and us sick.

Ticks cause local inflammation at the site of the bite, associated with the anti-coagulant the tick uses to suck blood. In severe cases, the blood loss can cause anemia. The tick bite can become infected. In rare cases, the Dermacentor tick can cause tick paralysis.

Tick-borne infections commonly seen in dogs are Lyme disease (*Borrelia burgdorferi*), anaplasmosis and ehrlichia. Dual and triple infections can occur at the same time. There are likely other tick-borne diseases that have not yet been identified. While it is believed it takes 48 hours of attachment for a tick to transmit Lyme disease, other infections can transmit in as little as three hours. Immature ticks are the most common lifecycle stage to transmit disease. The Ixodes ticks that transmit Lyme disease in their immature stage are very small and light colored, making detection on a dog difficult. These stages are most active in December through March, even in the upper Midwestern states at a time of year most people think tick control is unnecessary. Brown dog ticks can live year-round in homes and kennels.

Reactive or seasonal use of tick-control products allows home infestations to establish and allows transmission of disease because products are often not applied until tick activity has been observed. These are the reasons to use flea and tick control products year round. If tick control is not achieved using these products, permethrin or other pyrethroids can be sprayed into cracks and crevices, behind and under cages, and along the boards in the ceiling of the home and/or kennel.

Mites

There are four types of mites seen commonly in dogs: ear mites, scabies mites, Cheyletiella mites and demodex mites. Mites as a group cause a disorder of the skin known as mange.

Ear mites

A very common cause of ear infection in cats, these are less of a problem in dogs. Symptoms include head shaking, scratching and discharge from the ears. Without treatment, ear mites will continue to repopulate your pet's ears, leading to ongoing symptoms. Ear mites are easily diagnosed with an otoscope or under the microscope at your veterinarian's office.

The only approved product to control ear mites in dogs is Revolution. However, cleaning the ears and treating with medications to control the secondary yeast and bacterial infections will usually manage the condition. If one pet in the household has mites, they should all be treated. The best news is ear mites are rarely transmitted to humans.

Scabies mites

These sarcoptic mange mites are highly contagious but very difficult to find and diagnose. Also known as "red mange," they live deep in the hair follicles, causing intense scratching and hair loss, with most severe lesions on the edges of the dog's ears as well as the elbows. However, they can live anywhere on the skin, and over time can populate the entire body, causing generalized scratching, rash and hair loss.

Because scabies mites can be hard to find on skin scraping (an in-office test done at your veterinary clinic), they often go undiagnosed, sometimes leading to a lifetime of presumed allergies or other untreated skin disease. Until recently, treatment could be a challenge. However, Revolution (labeled for scabies) and some of the newer oral flea and tick medications (although not labeled to manage scabies mites) do a great job of killing the mites. A minimum of two treatments are required to eliminate the adult mites and the new mites that hatch after treatment. With these new oral flea and tick medications in the isoxazoline group, dogs are less likely to develop sarcoptic mange because many will be treated (even if you are using it to manage flea and tick populations) and the disorder controlled before they develop symptoms.

Because these are contagious, you should treat all of the dogs in the household, even if just one appears to have sarcoptic mange. These mites can be picked up at the groomers, anywhere the dog is in contact with other dogs, as well as from wild canids. People can transiently find themselves bitten by scabies mites, but dog scabies won't stay on a human long, only long enough to cause a rash. Human scabies is a different mite that requires treatment from your physician.

Cheyletiella Mites

This type of mite is also known as "walking dandruff" or the hair-clasping mite. Unlike demodectic and sarcoptic mites, which live in the hair follicles, this mite lives on the skin surface. With young eyes or magnification, these mites can be seen moving on the dog's skin. They are contagious dog to dog by direct contact with an infected dog. Because of this, they are most often seen on puppies and young dogs who have been housed in larger facilities such as breeding colonies and rescue facilities. Humans may briefly develop a rash, but will not have a long-term infestation.

There is no approved treatment for this mite. However, a number of different treatments have been shown to be effective, including high-dose ivermectin (avoid in MDR1 deficient dogs), milbemycin oxime (Interceptor and Sentinel), moxidectin (Simparica and Proheart), selamectin (Revolution), fipronil (Frontline) and pyrethrin shampoos. Monthly retreatment or reapplication of these products will provide long-term control.

Demodex Mites

Demodex mites can cause a disorder, demodicosis or demodectic mange, that can lead to hair loss. Small numbers of mites are considered normal skin critters, but when the dog's immune system is lacking, mange can result. There are two forms of demodectic mange: localized (small number of small patches, usually on the head and legs) and generalized (when large patches of hair loss develop). All puppies are exposed shortly after birth, but most dogs with a healthy immune system will have only low numbers of demodex in their hair follicles and will not develop associated skin lesions.

Unlike sarcoptic mange, demodex rarely causes dogs to feel itchy unless there is a secondary infection. Both forms of demodectic mange affect puppies under six months of age more commonly than adults. However, adults, particularly if they have an immune deficiency such as Cushing's disease, poor nutrition, chemotherapy or steroid use, may also develop demodectic mange.

Demodex is diagnosed on skin scraping, a test done in the office at your veterinary clinic, or on skin biopsy. Unlike sarcoptic mange, demodex mites are easier to find. Sometimes, these mites are seen during fecal examination. Humans will not become infected by canine demodex.

There currently are no approved drugs to treat demodex. Localized demodex often resolves on its own; generalized can require long-term treatment. Comprehensive treatment should include use of an effective miticide; evaluation for any underlying disorders and appropriate treatment when found; antibiotic therapy when pyoderma is present, and spaying of females to prevent recurrence during subsequent heat cycles.

Although there is no approved treatment in the United States for demodex, isoxazolines can be effective and simple treatments. All four of the current drugs in this new drug class are safe and effective (avoid in seizure-prone dogs), but should be used for the lifetime of the dog to prevent recurrence. Ivermectin (not for MDR1 deficient dogs), milbemycin (Interceptor and Sentinel) and moxidectin (Proheart 6 and 12) have also been shown to be effective, although not approved for demodex in dogs in the United States. There is a suspicion demodectic mange has a genetic tendency, but a clear link has not been established.

21. Flea and Tick Primer

There are three classes of flea and tick meds:

Route of administration	Advantages	Disadvantages	Product names
Topical	1. Permethrins repel fleas, ticks and other flying/biting insects like biting flies and mosquitoes. 2. Some are approved for breeding dogs.	1. Greasy spot at application site. 2. "Heebie-jeebies" in few patients as product dries. 3. Exposure of kids and cats.	1. Vectra 3D 2. Advantage 3. Frontline 4. Too many to list
Oral	1. Kills fleas and ticks within 24 hours of biting, in time to prevent tick-borne disease transmission. 2. Bravecto – approved for breeding males and females. 3. No exposure to others (children, elderly, cats) in home. 4. No skin irritation.	1. No biting-insect repellency. 2. Some patients have tremors. 3. Isoxazolines are not recommended for seizure-prone patients. 4. Bravecto – not approved for dogs < 6 months due to changing body size/weight.	1. Bravecto 2. Nexgard 3. Credelio 4. Simparica
Collar	Easy to apply. Traditional way to control fleas and ticks.	1. Not approved for breeding male and female dogs in the U.S. 2. Flea/tick repellency.	1. Seresto

Flea/Tick/Heartworm Products With Efficacy And Safety Information

Product	Active Ingredients	Purpose/Effective Against
HEARTWORM PREVENTION		
Advantage Multi for Dogs	Imidacloprid and moxidectin	Flea, louse, heartworm, hookworm, whipworm, roundworm and mange. Topical every 30 days.
Heartgard Plus	Ivermectin, Pyrantel pamoate	Heartworm, roundworms and hookworms. Tablet every 30 days.
Heartgard	Ivermectin	Heartworm. Tablet every 30 days
Interceptor	Milbemycin oxime	Heartworm, hookworm, whipworm and roundworm. Tablet every 30 days.
Interceptor Plus	Milbemycin oxime and praziquantel tablet	Heartworm, roundworm, adult hookworm, adult whipworm and adult tapeworm. Tablet every 30 days.
Iverhart Max	Ivermectin, Pyrantel pamoate, praziquantel	Heartworm, roundworms, hookworms and tapeworms. Tablet every 30 days.
Iverhart Plus	Ivermectin, Pyrantel pamoate	Heartworm, roundworms and hookworms. Chewable tablet every 30 days.
ProHeart 6	Moxidectin	Prevention of heartworm disease. Treatment of existing larval and adult hookworms. Injection at your veterinarian every 6 months.

Minimum Age/Weight	Pregnant/Nursing/Male Per Package Label
7 weeks/3 lbs	Safety not established.
6 weeks	Safe in pregnant or breeding females, stud dogs.
6 weeks	Safe in pregnant or breeding females, stud dogs.
4 weeks/2 lbs	Safe.
Dogs and puppies 2 pounds of body weight or greater and 6 weeks of age and older.	Safe. Not evaluated in breeding, pregnant or lactating dogs. Only milbemycin has been studied and is safe.
8 weeks/6 lbs	Not evaluated in pregnant or lactating females. Safe in males.
6 weeks	Safe in pregnant or breeding females, stud dogs.
6 months and older. Test prior to administration.	Not defined but assume same as Proheart 12.

Product	Active Ingredients	Purpose/Effective Against
HEARTWORM PREVENTION		
ProHeart 12	Moxidectin	Prevention of heartworm disease. Treatment of existing larval and adult hookworms. Injection at your veterinarian every 12 months.
Revolution	Selamectin	Heartworm, fleas, flea eggs, scabies mites, ear mites, hookworms, roundworms, lice and ticks. Topical every 30 days.
Sentinel	Milbemycin, Lufenuron	Heartworm, roundworms, whipworms, hookworms and flea eggs. Tablet every 30 days.
Sentinel Spectrum	Milbemycin, Lufenuron, Praziquantel	Heartworm, roundworms, whipworms, hookworms and flea eggs and tapeworms. Tablet every 30 days.
Tri-Heart Plus	Ivermectin, Pyrantel pamoate	Heartworm, roundworms and hookworms. Chewable tablet every 30 days.
Trifexis	Milbemycin oxime and Spinosad	Heartworm, fleas, roundworms, hookworms and whipworms. Tablet every 30 days.

Minimum Age/Weight	Pregnant/Nursing/Male Per Package Label
12 months and older. Test prior to administration.	Breeding females: No adverse effects in terms of conception, pregnancy maintenance, and the development, growth and health of the puppies were observed through puppy weaning at 6 weeks of age. Breeding males: No clinically significant changes or abnormalities were noted in semen quality.
6 weeks	To prevent roundworm infection, Revolution should be administered at monthly intervals during pregnancy with a dose administered approximately 2 weeks before parturition. The next treatment should be administered to the female 10 days after parturition and followed by another treatment 1 month later. This schedule of treatments for females will prevent adult roundworm infections in suckling puppies for 7 weeks after birth.
4 weeks & 2 lbs	Safe.
6 weeks & 2 lbs	Not tested
6 weeks	Safe.
8 weeks & 5 lbs	Not safe in pregnancy due to fetal malformations, not evaluated in males. Caution in dogs with seizure history. Use with caution in breeding females.

Product	Active Ingredients	Purpose/Effective Against
FLEA AND TICK PREVENTION		
Activyl Protector Band for Dogs	Deltamethrin	Fleas and ticks. Repels mosquitoes. Collar, use every 6 months. Water resistant. 21 days to maximum efficacy.
Activyl Topical	Indoxacarb & Permethrin	Fleas. Topical, every 30 days.
Advantage II	Imidacloprid & insect growth regulator (pyriproxyfen)	Adult fleas, flea larvae, flea eggs, lice. Topical, every 30 days.
BioGroom	Pyrethrin shampoo	Kills fleas, ticks, lice and ear mites. Shampoo and spray, every 30 days.
BioSpot Active Care Spot on	Etofenprox, Piperonyl, Pyriproxyfen (Nylar®) (S)-Methoprene	Fleas, flea eggs, flea larvae, tick, tick nymphs, tick larvae, brown dog ticks, deer ticks. Kills and repels mosquitoes Topical, every 30 days.
Bravecto	Fluralaner	Fleas, ticks 12 weeks black-legged tick, American dog tick, and brown dog tick), and for 8 weeks Lone star tick). Topical.
Bravecto Puppy 1 month	Fluralaner	

Minimum Age/Weight	Pregnant/Nursing/Male Per Package Label
12 weeks & 4 lbs	Consult a veterinarian before using this product on pregnant, medicated or nursing animals.
8 weeks & 4 lbs	Do not use on dogs (male or female) intended for breeding, or on dogs that are pregnant or nursing.
3 lbs & 7 weeks	Consult your veterinarian before using this product on debilitated, aged, pregnant or nursing dogs.
5 lbs & 12 weeks	Consult a veterinarian before using on sick, aged pregnant or nursing animals.
12 weeks	Do not use.
6 months/4.4 lbs	There were no clinically relevant, treatment-related effects on the body weights, food consumption, reproductive performance, semen analysis, litter data, gross necropsy (adult dogs) or histopathology findings (adult dogs and puppies). Bravecto has not been shown to be effective for 12-weeks duration in puppies less than 6 months of age. Use with caution in dogs with a history of seizures.

Product	Active Ingredients	Purpose/Effective Against
FLEA AND TICK PREVENTION		
Capstar tabs	Nitenpyram	Fleas as often as 1 x a day.
Certifect	Fipronil, Amitraz and S-methoprene	Deer ticks, Gulf Coast ticks, black legged ticks, brown dog ticks, American dog ticks, Lone Star ticks, yellow dog ticks, European dog ticks, wood ticks and paralysis ticks. Topical, every 30 days.
Comfortis	Spinosad	Fleas. Tablet every 30 days.
Credelio	Lotilaner	Adult fleas and Lone star tick, American dog tick, Black-legged tick and brown dog tick. Tablet every 30 days.
EFFIPRO Plus Topical Solution	Fipronil and pyriproxyfen	Fleas, ticks, mosquitoes and chewing lice. Every 30 days.
EFFITIX Topical Solution	Fipronil & permethrin	Fleas, flea eggs, flea pupae, flea larvae, ticks and mosquitoes. Topical every 30 days.
FiproGuard	Fipronil & s-methoprene	Fleas and ticks. Topical every 30 days.
FiproGuard Plus	Fipronil, (s)-methoprene	Fleas, ticks and lice. Topical every 30 days.
Frontline	Fipronil	Fleas, ticks and chewing lice. Waterproof. Topical every 30 days.
Frontline Plus	Fipronil and (S)-methoprene	Fleas including eggs and larvae, ticks, mites/mange, and lice. Waterproof. Topical every 30 days.

Minimum Age/Weight	Pregnant/Nursing/Male Per Package Label
4 weeks/2 lbs	Birth defects and fetal loss
5 pounds & 8 weeks	Can also be used on breeding pregnant and lactating females.
3.3 pounds & 14 weeks	Caution in dogs with seizure history. Safety has not been evaluated in breeding males. Use with caution in breeding females.
8 weeks of age & 4.4 pounds	The safe use of Credelio in breeding, pregnant or lactating dogs has not been evaluated. Use with caution in dogs with a history of seizures.
8 weeks & 5 lbs	Do not use on pregnant or lactating dogs.
8 weeks	Consult a veterinarian before using on pregnant or nursing dogs.
8 weeks	Safe for breeding, pregnant and lactating dogs.
Dog: 8 weeks	Safe for breeding, pregnant and lactating dogs.
8 weeks	Can be used on breeding, pregnant and lactating females.
Dog: 8 weeks/5 lbs	Safe for breeding, pregnant and lactating dogs.

Product	Active Ingredients	Purpose/Effective Against
FLEA AND TICK PREVENTION		
Frontline Spray	Fipronil	Fleas, ticks and chewing lice. Kills all life stages of ticks (larva, nymph and adult), including brown dog ticks American dog ticks, Lone star ticks and Deer ticks. Wear gloves. Approximately 1 to 2 pumps per pound of the animal's body weight will be required. Pets with long or dense coats will require the higher rate. Waterproof. Spray 30 to 90 days.
Frontline Gold	Fipronil, (s)-methoprene, and pyriproxyfen	Flea, tick and chewing lice. Topical every 30 days.
Hartz First Defense	Fipronil	Fleas, ticks and chewing lice. Waterproof. Topical every 30 days.
K9 Advantix II	Imidacloprid, Permethrin and Pyriproxyfen	Ticks, fleas, mosquitoes, biting flies and lice. Topical every 30 days, can reapply in 7 days.
Nexgard	Afoxolaner	Fleas and ticks. Chewable tablet every 30 days.
Parastar	Fipronil	Fleas and ticks. Topical every 30 days.
PetArmor	Fipronil	Fleas and ticks. Topical every 30 days.
PetArmor Plus for Dogs	Fipronil and S-Methoprene	Adult fleas, flea eggs, flea larvae, ticks, chewing lice and prevents the development of flea pupae. It controls mites that may cause sarcoptic mange and kills deer ticks that can transmit Lyme disease. It also kills brown dog ticks, American dog ticks and Lone star ticks, and prevents flea reinfestations for 4 weeks. Topical.

Minimum Age/Weight	Pregnant/Nursing/Male Per Package Label
8 weeks	Approved for use on all dogs, including breeding, pregnant, and lactating females and puppies as young as 8 weeks.
Dog: 8 weeks/5lbs	Safe.
8 weeks	Safe for breeding, pregnant and lactating females.
7 weeks/4 lbs	Consult your veterinarian before using this product on debilitated, aged, pregnant or nursing animals.
8 weeks & 4 lbs	Not tested. Caution in dogs with seizure history.
8 weeks	Safe for breeding, pregnant and lactating dogs.
8 weeks	Safe for breeding, pregnant and lactating dogs.
8 weeks	Safe for breeding, pregnant and lactating dogs.

Product	Active Ingredients	Purpose/Effective Against
FLEA AND TICK PREVENTION		
Preventic Collar	Amitraz	Collar. Ticks for 90 days.
Revolution	Selamectin	Heartworm, fleas and flea eggs, ear mites, Sarcoptes, American Dog Tick. Topical every 30 days.
Scalibor Protector Band collar	Deltamethrin	Fleas & ticks. Collar every 6 months.
Sentry Capguard	Nitenpyram	Fleas as often as 1 x a day. Tablet.
Sentry FiproGuard Plus for Dogs	Fipronil and S-Methoprene	Adult fleas, flea eggs, flea larvae, ticks, chewing lice and prevents the development of flea pupae. It controls mites that may cause sarcoptic mange and kills deer ticks that can transmit Lyme disease. It also kills Brown Dog, American dog and Lone Star ticks, and prevents flea reinfestations for 4 weeks. Topical.
Sentry Natural Defense	Peppermint oil, cinnamon oil, lemongrass oil, clove oil and thyme oil.	Fleas, ticks and mosquitoes. Topical every 30 days.
Seresto collar	Flumethrin and Imidacloprid	Fleas, ticks, lice, sarcoptic mites. Collar, 8 months.

Minimum Age/Weight	Pregnant/Nursing/Male Per Package Label
12 weeks	Not tested.
Dog: 6 weeks Cat: 8 weeks	Safe.
12 weeks	Consult a veterinarian before using this product on debilitated, aged, pregnant, medicated or nursing animals.
2 pounds & 4 weeks	Birth defects and fetal loss.
8 weeks	Safe for breeding, pregnant and lactating dogs.
12 weeks	Attacks octopamine. Consult your veterinarian.
7 weeks and 18 pounds	Consult your veterinarian before using this product on debilitated, aged, breeding, pregnant or nursing animals.

Product	Active Ingredients	Purpose/Effective Against
FLEA AND TICK PREVENTION		
Simparica	Sarolaner	Adult fleas, and is indicated for the treatment and prevention of flea infestations and the treatment and control of tick infestations Lone Star, Gulf Coast, American dog and brown dog ticks. Chewable tablet every 30 days.
Spectra Shield medallion	Zetacy-permethrin & Piperonyl Butoxide	Fleas and ticks. Tag on a collar. Lasts up to 4 months.
Vectra 3D	Dinotefuran, Pyriproxyfen, & Permethrin	Fleas and ticks. Every 30 days. Mosquito and biting flies, sand mites, lice repellency. Water repellency. "Hot foot" effect before they bite. Topical.
Vet's Best Natural Flea & Tick spot-on	Clove Leaf Oil, Thyme White Oil, Cinnamon Oil	Fleas and ticks, repels mosquitoes. Topical.
HEARTWORM AND FLEA/TICK IN COMBINATION		
Simparica Trio	Sarolaner, moxidectin, and pyrantel chewable tablets	Prevention of heartworm disease, treatment and control of roundworms and hookworms. Kills adult fleas, treats and controls ticks (Lone Star tick, Gulf Coast tick, American dog tick, black-legged tick, and brown dog tick). Chewable tablet every 30 days.

Minimum Age/Weight	Pregnant/Nursing/Male Per Package Label
6 months & 2.8 pounds	Not tested. Use with caution in dogs with a history of seizures.
6 months	If used on pregnant or nursing dogs, do not replace medallion until puppies are at least 6 weeks old.
8 weeks & 2.5 pounds	Do not use in animals used for breeding.
12 weeks	Label is silent.
1 month in dogs and puppies > 8 weeks and older > 2.8 pounds	

CHAPTER 12

Emergency Care

Emergencies can't be scheduled, budgeted or planned for. In today's COVID-19 era, one chance meeting with an infected person can land you in the ICU on a ventilator. And one slip of your new puppy out the front door and into traffic could land your dog in intensive care at the emergency animal hospital.

Without planning and insurance, you or your pet can have a catastrophically terrible outcome. No one can predict what might happen next. And no one can prevent every crisis. But you can do your best to plan ahead to mitigate the likelihood you will lose your beloved dog to a crisis.

The most common causes of accidental death in puppies are:

- Intestinal blockage

- Ingesting toxins

- Being hit by a car or other serious trauma

All three scenarios are dangerous, painful, expensive – and preventable with appropriate supervision, prepping your home and using a leash appropriately. Please don't let this happen to *your* new puppy.

Vomiting

Vomiting is one of the most common problems for which dogs see their veterinarian. Dogs are willing to eat almost anything, even lots of things that are not edible or good for them. You may have seen evidence that your dog consumed something that is a clear cause of vomiting – whether spoiled food, bones, fatty food or an inedible object. This information must be shared with your veterinary professional.

When a dog swallows a large object, it will usually make it into the stomach. However, it may not make it all the way through the intestinal tract. These inedible items include towels, socks, plastic and toys. When

PET INSURANCE

This is a volatile market that changes too fast and in scope to make specific recommendations. Pet health insurance has a monthly premium. Some plans are more comprehensive than others. One size doesn't fit all.

The only pet owners who don't need insurance are rich ones. The rest of us should investigate the practicality of having insurance.

Research online and by phone before making a decision: www.avma.org/resources/pet-owners/petcare/do-you-need-pet-insurance.

Consider only "major medical" coverage – for those occurrences you hope never happen.

With health problems that are catastrophic, life threatening and too expensive to come out of your monthly cash flow, insurance can make all the difference. Insurance can be life saving for your pet. This includes trauma such as being hit by a car, orthopedic problems such as hip dysplasia and torn cruciate ligaments, ingestion of foreign material requiring surgery, and cancer.

Ask about what is pre-existing, inherited, genetic or otherwise not covered.

Routine care such as vaccinations and parasite protection are not a bargain for insured pets – you are better off to budget for these.

there is a mismatch of size between the item swallowed and the size of the puppy, this item is likely to cause a bowel obstruction, requiring surgery for removal.

One or two episodes of productive vomiting (meaning the puppy vomited something up) is not reason to panic. However, if the vomiting persists, contains blood, or your dog is distressed, a veterinary visit should be scheduled.

There are few over-the-counter products that help reduce vomiting. There are several very good prescription medications that can be effective. In many cases, diagnostic testing, including blood tests and imaging (ultrasound and/or X-ray), are indicated to determine the underlying cause. Vomiting without diarrhea is usually an indicator of a more serious illness than when the puppy has diarrhea and vomiting.

Withholding food (but not water) for a short time, until you can get in to see the veterinarian, is helpful. Continue to offer small amounts of water or ice cubes to keep your pet hydrated until the visit. Using human medications or prescriptions for another pet is not recommended. Oral medications to control vomiting often fail – if the puppy can't keep the medication down, the medication won't work. Your veterinarian will likely use injectable medications, fluids and a diet change.

If you see more than two or three episodes of vomiting, if the vomiting is unproductive (i.e., nothing comes up), the puppy is not passing stools, or you believe your puppy swallowed a foreign object, see your veterinarian.

Diarrhea

Diarrhea is not as serious as vomiting. However, diarrhea can be messier and more distressing to you than to your dog. Accidents on the carpet or hourly trips outside in the middle of the night are hard on you. Most puppies won't have a stool in their crate, but if they have diarrhea, they are unlikely to be able to prevent an accident.

Many times, vomiting and diarrhea happen at the same or similar time. As with vomiting, many times you have witnessed something that suggests a diagnosis of the cause of diarrhea. This is important information to share with your veterinary professional. Diarrhea followed by vomiting is usually not as serious as vomiting alone.

A little diarrhea is not dangerous to your pet. However, severe diarrhea, vomiting and diarrhea, or large volumes of blood in the diarrhea are reason to see the veterinarian as soon as possible.

There are not many over-the-counter medications that work well, but there are great prescription drugs to return your pet's stools to normal. Real kaolin-pectin (not human Kaopectate) works well. Imodium is safe but many dogs vomit after taking this medication. Most other human medications should not be shared with your puppy or dog.

Diarrhea is common in puppies. It can create a major setback in housebreaking and crate training. Be patient, keep the puppy off the new carpet, and keep him well hydrated.

Fasting for 12 to 24 hours (don't take water away) or a bland diet can help resolve the diarrhea. Canned pumpkin, boiled hamburger and rice, and yogurt are all useful home remedies. If these techniques fail, contact your veterinarian for more advanced medical care.

Foreign Bodies

In a dog, nearly anything that isn't food and can be swallowed can become a foreign body. Some of the most frequently seen foreign objects consumed by dogs are smelly things, especially things that carry the scent of their favorite person – cell phones, TV remote controls, underwear, socks, dish towels, pieces of rugs, baby and children's toys, and on and on. In dogs, just because they can swallow it doesn't mean it will pass through the intestines. The worst foreign bodies are "linear"– balloon strings, pantyhose and rug strings. Linear foreign bodies can do much more damage – they get caught as they are passing and saw through the intestines, especially if they are caught around the base of the tongue.

Preventing foreign bodies is as simple as not letting the dog get into anything. Easier said than done, especially if there are either little children or forgetful adults in the home who undo what you try to do to keep the dog safe. Teach your children to put their dirty laundry in a covered bin, not to leave backpacks in reach of the dog, and to pick up little toy pieces when the dog is in the room.

If your puppy starts vomiting, quickly scout the house for foreign bodies and potentially toxic substances before you head to the veterinarian's office. If you suspect one of these, take along a sample to help your veterinary team make a diagnosis.

Toxins

There are many toxins in your home. Some are obviously dangerous, such cleaning products. Others – including grapes, raisins, chocolate, macadamia nuts, ibuprofen, and sugarless gum and candy containing xylitol – may come as more of a surprise to owners.

BLEEDING

Bleeding always seems worse when it is your blood or the blood of someone you love. The same holds true with puppies, especially when they dart though the house, leaving prints wherever they go.

First, catch the puppy to minimize clean-up. If all else fails, pop him into a crate to control the situation. Then, with care, evaluate the situation. If it is a bleeding nail, use flour or styptic powder on the nail tip, then cover it with a sock that you tape over the foot. If anything else is bleeding, use plastic food wrap, a T-shirt or a sock to cover the source of the injury and transport your puppy to the veterinary clinic, after you call to let them know you are on your way.

- **Xylitol.** Xylitol is the component of many sugarless gums and candies. While safe for humans, at relatively small doses it can cause low blood sugar and liver damage in dogs. Commonly, these are in backpacks, purses and stashes of small children, and are ingested without your knowledge. Rarely, xylitol is in high-end peanut butter and certain human nutritional supplements as a sweetener. Symptoms include staggering, confusion and seizures. Treatment includes supportive care, ice cream when en route to the veterinarian (to keep your puppy's blood sugar high enough to prevent seizures until you can get veterinary help) and immediate veterinary intervention.

- **Marijuana.** Yes, dogs will eat marijuana, straight from the bag or in other forms such as brownies and other edibles like gummies. Dogs will find it hidden under the bed, in a jacket pocket, or in a dresser drawer or backpack. Frequently, family members are unaware of the stash until the dog presents with a toxicity.

CHOKING

Fortunately, puppies don't usually choke on food or other objects. However, you can use a Heimlich maneuver on the puppy if he starts to choke. Avoid sticking your fingers into the throat, as you are likely to get bitten, sometimes badly. Additionally, you may force the item further back into the puppy's throat.

The Heimlich is done on a dog like a human except the dog is horizontal. Standing over the puppy, facing his head, put both hands under the end of the rib cage, and forcefully thrust upward. It is OK to repeat this if needed. If you have a smaller puppy, you can pick him up and use a forceful pat on the back with his head down to try to dislodge the foreign object.

Symptoms include drowsiness, staggering or stumbling, vomiting, tremors, dilated or constricted pupils, low body temperature, crying, excessive salivation, excessive urination and, if severe, coma. Veterinary intervention, including urine testing to confirm a diagnosis and supportive care, is essential.

- **Rodenticides.** There are several active ingredients in rat and mouse poisons on the market. The most common is a vitamin K antagonist, leading to bleeding disorders and death if not diagnosed and treated. One of the newer poisons is a vitamin D compound that drives the calcium up, causing kidney failure. The only great thing about this toxin is the mouse or rat that ingests it gets thirsty and comes out of hiding to look for a drink before it dies, so you don't find a skeleton in the closet. The bad news is it is highly toxic to dogs and children.

Instead of the usual rat and mouse poisons that are toxic, use one that contains only corn gluten. This kills mice and rats by causing bowel obstruction but is not toxic so it is safe around children and pets.

Trauma

There are more kinds of trauma that can happen to a dog than can be listed here. Even when you are careful, bad things happen. First, remember puppies are intensely curious and faster than a greased pig. So keep your puppy away from anything you even remotely think can go wrong, especially slipping out a gate or door when you least expect it.

If your puppy is in an accident, seek immediate veterinary care. As with people, trauma that doesn't seem or look serious can turn out to have grave consequences. When in doubt, take the puppy in for an evaluation. You will sleep better and may save your puppy's life.

How do I muzzle my dog?

In the unfortunate event your dog is injured and is frantically trying to bite anyone who comes near, you may need to know how to put on a muzzle. Anything that is long and skinny, like a leash, belt or pantyhose, can be used as a muzzle.

There are three steps to tying a muzzle, after finding supplies and getting close enough to the dog to safely place a muzzle.

First, make a loop in your muzzle material, and carefully advance it over the dog's muzzle/bridge of her nose. Tie the loop snugly enough to keep the dog's jaws closed.

The second step is to tie a loop under the jaw, just under the tied loop over the bridge of the dog's nose.

Third, tie a bow (never a knot, in case you have to get it off quickly) behind the dog's ears. This requires a fairly long bit of leash to work. It will not work on a short-faced dog like a Pug or Bulldog. In those cases, you may need to use a heavy towel or blanket over the dog's head to protect you from him swinging it to bite at you, even when you are the one trying to help.

Avoid muzzling the dog if he is vomiting or having difficulty breathing.

Before moving the dog for transport, cover any open wound – food plastic wrap will work. Immobilize any leg fracture if possible. There are no neck braces for dogs; if you suspect a neck or back injury, keep the dog's spine as straight as possible.

Once the dog is safely muzzled, with all wounds managed, use a heavy blanket or board/cardboard as a stretcher. Carefully lift the dog into a vehicle for transport to veterinary care. Remember to call the veterinary clinic in advance so they are prepared to help you on arrival.

Planning for Your Absence

The sad, harsh reality is that sometimes we have an unplanned absence from our pets. This may be temporary or permanent. It may involve only you – especially worrisome if you are the sole caretaker for your pets. It may involve your entire family if there is a terrible catastrophe.

The best advice here is to have a written plan in place. A "will" takes months, even years to be activated. A better plan is to have a "trust "or other plan in place. Your pets can't wait more than a few hours for you to return, so the process has to be seamless.

To have a great plan, you must plan in advance. You may want to reciprocate with a friend, family member or co-worker: Agree that you will help with their pet care and they will help with yours in return. Even better, have a primary plan with a secondary one, in case the first plan falls apart.

To make this work, have the plan in writing and keep it updated, both in writing and in verbal communication. Be sure your pet's medical needs will be met. Have medical records, medications, prescription foods and veterinary contact information available. Consider having a joint checking account with a little bit of money set aside in it – a portion from you and a portion from your co-planner so that immediate medical needs can be funded. This won't take a lot of money – just enough that you don't have to worry.

If the dogs are valuable as show or breeding dogs, and/or if you have a larger group of dogs, consider a co-ownership agreement, drafted by an attorney who understands animal law. By doing this, should your dogs be seized by animal control, ownership can shift to your co-planner immediately, and your dogs released to your co-planner before they can be spayed or neutered, and placed as pets where you will never have a chance to get them back.

You may think this could never happen to you. But we are all just one car accident or one stroke away from losing our beloved dogs. All you have to do is not provide care for a very short time, and, poof, your dogs are gone, confiscated by animal control with or without legal authority, and placed in homes where they will never return to you.

For professional legal assistance with this, visit https://hamiltonlawandmediation.com.

What is "normal"?

- **Hiccups** – Young puppies commonly have hiccups. It's nothing to be concerned about.

- **Dream sleeping** – Many puppies have "running" motions with their feet and legs when sleeping. Again: Completely normal.

- **Humping** – Humping other dogs, kids, pillows and other objects is a common puppy behavior. It is a status behavior, not a sexual one, seen in both males and females, neutered, spayed and intact. This behavior should be discouraged by distracting the puppy. Be careful the distraction is not a "reward" that encourages future humping behavior.

- **Zoomies at night** – There are many puppies that have the "zoomies" in the evening. This is a lot like children who become overactive when overtired. The best way to manage this is to keep puppies exercised and alert during the evening hours, so that at bedtime they are willing to sleep, crated or not.

Your Pet's First-Aid Kit

Item	Use or Purpose
Daily medication	Check for expiration dates.
Waterproof container	Storage.
First-aid book	
Vet's phone number	Emergency assistance.
Poison control number	National Animal Poison Control: 1-888-426-4435
Hemostat	To remove ticks, porcupine quills, fish hooks, etc.
Super glue	To repair small cuts on foot pads and torn nails.
Eye wash	To wash eyes free of foreign materials and irritants.
Antibiotic eye ointment	To treat minor eye irritation.
Ear wash	To clean and flush ears after swimming and bathing.
Pain medication for pets	To treat aches and pains but *no* Ibuprofen.
Nail trimmer	To trim torn, long or jagged nails.
Skunk odor eliminator	Skunk Stuff or the makings for baking soda, hydrogen peroxide and dish soap.
Rectal thermometer	To detect fevers, colds and overheating. (Normal is 101-102.5.)

Instant cold pack	To control swelling caused by injury, insect bites and burns.
Calorie supplement	An energy supplement to prevent overtiring.
Latex exam gloves	For safe handling of wounds.
Cotton swabs or Q-Tips	For cleaning ears and wounds.
Elastic bandaging **1-inch adhesive tape** **Sterile Telfa pads** **Roll gauze** **Plastic wrap**	For wound care.
Pepcid tablets	For upset stomach.
Blanket	For protection or to use as a stretcher.
Fork	To remove burrs.
Flashlight	For better visibility.
Prednisone, Benadryl®	For allergic reactions
Stethoscope	Assessment.
Bloat kit	Includes stomach tube and mouth gag; use only if trained
Canned spinach	To feed if your dog eats small, sharp, inedible objects like screws or pens.

CHAPTER 13

Technology

In the era of COVID-19, many of us have learned new ways to work, communicate, take classes, hold meetings, visit family and friends, and shop – all while staying safe. Even some veterinary visits and puppy classes can happen virtually. While we can't and shouldn't replace every in-person communication, there are times electronic communication has real advantages – especially during a pandemic.

Other advantages include saving time, not waiting in the vet hospital for your appointment, and not having to fight traffic to get there and back. Some people actually prefer staying in their car for curbside service, using virtual communication while their pet receives veterinary care.

Telehealth

Just as you can do a virtual visit with your health-care provider, you and your dog can video-conference or message with your veterinarian. Cool, right? With video-conferencing, your vet can see your pet's skin problem or lameness, observe movement or behavior problems, look at a post-op incision or assess a lump.

The same applies to messaging. Not only does it allow for the sharing of text, videos and pictures, but doesn't require you and the vet to be present at the same time, and helps overcome glitching issues with live video and bandwidth. Messaging also allows you to capture that exact moment when your dog is exhibiting a worrisome behavior that he never manages to exhibit while in the vet office or on live video.

You can record videos of limping, seizures or other fleeting abnormalities so you can show or send them to your veterinary or behavioral professional. Nearly everyone has a cell phone with a camera. Train yourself to reach for your phone when you see something out of the ordinary. By archiving the activity or event, you can share it and improve your chances at an accurate diagnosis.

In many states, veterinarians who have a pre-existing "Valid Veterinary Client-Patient Relationship" (Valid VCPR) may be allowed to use telemedicine. This means if your veterinarian, you and your dog have had a recent in-person visit, you have a Valid VCPR. This is the legal requirement that your veterinarian is obligated to follow. If your veterinarian has sufficient knowledge of your pet's condition based on recent examination and will accept responsibility for decision-making, and if you as the pet owner agree to follow your vet's recommendations, you may be able to have a telemedicine visit.

When a Valid VCPR is in place, your veterinarian may be comfortable with a virtual visit. By video-conferencing, telephone consultation or messaging with you, your veterinarian may be able to prescribe treatment options for your dog. These can happen in real time or by email, text messaging or Facebook messages. The challenge is that your veterinarian can't do a hands-on evaluation. But in some cases, seeing video of your pet in his environment or showing specific episodes of activity can make for an even more accurate diagnosis than can be made in person.

The American Veterinary Medical Association outlines state-imposed requirements and limitations for virtual veterinary care at www.avma.org/sites/default/files/2019-12/VCPR-State-Chart-2019.pdf.

Veterinarians likely have a fee for telehealth services. The advantage is that you save time traveling to and from the veterinary hospital, as well as time waiting there, and you eliminate exposure to possible infectious diseases for both you and your dog.

Veterinary behaviorists are in a unique position to do virtual consultations. In most cases, a hands-on physical exam is not indicated. The behaviors your dog exhibits in your home, her natural environment, will be different that what would be seen at the behaviorist's office. By doing virtual visits, the veterinary behaviorist can assess behaviors and make recommendations to aid in treatment.

AirVet, Petzam, TeleTails, GuardianVets and other apps let you see your veterinarian and allow your vet to see you, your dog and the home environment. In real time, you can discuss your dog's health concerns, show your veterinarian what you are seeing, and have a "virtual" evaluation. In some cases, the evaluation can be done entirely over the app. Alternately, the app can be used for follow-up visits to check, for example, on how a surgical incision is healing or how lameness is resolving.

Your veterinary clinic can tell you which services they support. At the end of the call, your credit card is charged for the consultation fee.

TEXTING WITH YOUR VET

There are many communications you can manage with your veterinarian's staff. These include:

- An announcement that you and your pet have arrived for your curbside visit, and what make and model car, and parking spot, they can find you in.

- Requests for medication and pet-food refills.

- Prescriptions and diets ready for pick-up.

- "We left you a voice mail."

- "I am running late."

- Scheduling and rescheduling an appointment.

- Driving directions to the clinic.

- How-to video links – such as how to give a pill to your dog.

- Weather closures.

- Lab results.

- Pre-op and post-op instructions for care.

- Updates on hours, procedures and processes of the veterinary clinic.

Professional Telemedicine

For years, your veterinarian has been able to consult with other veterinary professionals to view X-rays, ultrasounds, EKGs and microscope slides of tissue samples. One of the most specialized services is Whelpwise, a veterinary monitoring service for dogs in labor.

Specialists in many veterinary disciplines can now contribute to your pet's veterinary care. With virtual consultations, your dog can "see" a radiologist, cardiologist, ophthalmologist, pathologist or other specialist without leaving your local veterinary clinic.

Ask your veterinary professionals if they provide these services. Again, keep in mind there will likely be a fee. But it is safer, more convenient and more efficient than a drive to see a veterinary specialist.

Veterinary Portals

Using a veterinary portal, you can easily access your pet's medical records stored in your veterinarian's computer database. This is useful when scheduling your next appointment, when you need to show proof of vaccinations for boarding, grooming or training classes, or in an emergency when you need to share information about the medications your pet has had prescribed. Many veterinary clinics now have portals. Just check their website or ask if they have this feature.

Doggie Wearables

This is the Apple Watch or Fitbit option for dogs. Whistle.com and Dogness, among others, allow you to monitor your dog's location, distance traveled, time active, calories burned and activity type, including running, walking, playing, resting, sleeping and scratching. This can help you assess if your dog is too active after surgery, too inactive and as a result risking weight gain, or too sore to move because of arthritis.

Invoicing for Vet Services

With COVID-19, curbside veterinary services have become the norm in many communities. To improve efficiency, and reduce waiting times, there is now software to allow you to invoice yourself for wellness services. These are routine immunizations and heartworm, flea and tick medications as well as heartworm and fecal testing. This software allows you to determine what services and products you want to purchase at your current visit, what you can afford during this pay period, and what rebates are available. Additionally, you can complete a questionnaire about your pet's health, food, treats and supplements while you are in your home, and can see what products you are using. If available, your veterinary clinic can help you with this service.

Medical Devices

- **Glucometers.** Some day our pets will be able to have implanted glucose monitors and insulin pumps. For now, there are pet-based glucometers. These meters can take a tiny drop of blood and test your dog's glucose level, allowing your vet to better manage his diabetes or low-blood-sugar condition. Be sure you talk to your veterinary professionals about how to incorporate this into your dog's treatment plan.

- **Pacemakers.** On rare occasions, a dog can have a heart condition that leads to a progressive slowing of the heart. Pacemakers inserted under the skin provide an electrical stimulus to the heart, keeping it beating at an appropriate rate. This is lifesaving for dogs with these electrical imbalances.

- **Force plate analysis.** This device, which looks like a digital scale, allows your veterinarian to assess how much weight your pet is bearing on each leg. This can help diagnose which leg he is lame on, and can be used to monitor progress after a surgical or medical procedure.

- **Laser surgery.** Using a surgical laser instead of a scalpel blade not only seals over blood vessels as the incision is made, it also reduces pain at the site of the surgical incision. This may have an additional fee associated with the surgical procedure, but for the sake of your pet's recovery, it is worth the extra money.

DNA ANALYSIS

There are currently three reasons to DNA-test your dog, depending on your goals:

- **Wisdom MX testing.** This and other DNA tests can determine what breeds of dogs were involved in making the amazing dog you are living with. There is little real benefit in knowing your dog's genetic make-up other than curiosity.

- **Parentage testing.** This can be used to determine the sire of your dog. (Because of the way canine reproduction works, any given litter can have two or more fathers involved.) In some cases, multiple males were used deliberately to accomplish a breeding. In others, the dogs "planned" their own breeding without the owner's consent – or knowledge. AKC, UKC and other registries require this testing when registering multiple-sire litters or if there is reason to believe that the presumed dad might turn out not to be.

- **Genetic disorder screening.** On a weekly basis, veterinarians are seeing new genetic DNA tests come to market. This is happening so fast that no one can keep up with all of these advances. If you know of a new test for your breed, help your veterinary professional become educated on it. There is very little oversight on testing development and accuracy. Some breeds are being tested for disorders not even recognized in that breed. Choose the lab you use carefully.

- **Laser therapy.** Using laser therapy, your veterinary professional can hasten healing from surgery or trauma, or speed up recovery from an ear infection. A series of treatments with this specialized light therapy may be recommended for your dog to achieve maximal benefit in her recovery.

- **CT and MRI scanners.** CT and MRI procedures are now available at many specialty centers. Use of these diagnostic techniques allow veterinarians to see brain tumors, torn ligaments and other pathology that can't be otherwise diagnosed without more invasive techniques.

- **3D printing.** As this technology advances, more and more uses are found. Shells and prosthetic limbs now allow for rehabilitation and recovery.

- **Joint replacements.** Hip replacements have been available for many years for medium- to large-breed dogs. This life-changing procedure can treat hip damage caused by hip dysplasia or trauma. Elbow and knee replacements are likely to become more available in the future.

- **Minimally invasive procedures/endoscopy.** There are many places that an endoscope can go to investigate body parts or treat pets. Scoping can be used to remove ingested foreign material, from socks to diamond rings, if they are still in the stomach. Scoping can be used to perform spays (ovariohysterectomies) through three small keyhole incisions, or locate tumors in nasal passages. All of these avoid surgeries or other invasive procedures.

- **Surgical monitors.** Gone are the days where monitoring your dog under anesthesia or after serious trauma involved only watch breathing and hearing the heartbeat with a stethoscope. Veterinarians can now monitor the EKG and respiration, the sPO2 (oxygenation of the blood), the amount of CO_2 in the air the dog exhales, and even blood pressure. Additionally, some of these monitors can transmit signals to another device using Bluetooth, so your dog can be monitored while the staff moves around the veterinary hospital. Monitoring can also be done remotely using cameras.

- **Ultrasounds.** Just as you can have an ultrasound done of your abdominal organs to monitor pregnancy or assess your heart (echocardiogram), veterinarians can offer the same services for their canine patients.

- **Holter monitor.** To assess heart rates and rhythms, veterinary professionals can now use a Holter monitor, a harness with monitor leads that your dog wears for 24 hours.

- **Vital signs.** Your veterinarian can collect heart rates and rhythms on a cell-phone device called AliveCor. With CardioPet, vets can transmit an EKG to cardiologists all over the country to assess your dog for heart disease. Vets can email digital X-rays and ultrasounds to veterinary radiologists, and even use artificial intelligence (AI) to have X-rays read by a computer.

Other Cool Technologies

- **Invisible Fences.** Some neighborhoods and developments don't allow physical fences. In these communities, an invisible fence can be your next best option. It requires placing a buried wire around the perimeter of the areas where you want the dog to have or not have access. The dog then wears a collar that emits a warning beep that he is crossing into forbidden territory; if he ignores it, the collar emits a mild but dissuasive electric shock. The disadvantages to an invisible fence are that it won't keep other animals out of the yard, training your dog to understand the boundaries takes time, and if your dog succumbs to temptation and chases the bunny anyway, the electric jolt on the way back in may deter your dog from returning home.

- **GPS tracking collars.** These smart collars allow you to track the location of your dog using an app on your cell phone. While primarily used by hunters, these collars can be used for any dog whose location needs to be tracked.

- **Managed feeders and doors.** With the simple addition of a computer chip in a tag on your pet's collar, your dog can come and go through a doggie door. Or he can have access or be blocked access at a food dish. The computer chip allows only the tagged pet in through the door or into the feeder, blocking others.

- **Camera monitors.** Cameras, standing alone or as part of a surveillance system, are increasingly available and affordable. You can observe your puppy or dog from your cell phone or your computer from remote locations in your home, your desk at work or while you are out of town. While it's great to be able to see what your dog does in your absence, it can be upsetting if you can't do anything from where you are to "fix" any problems.

- **Interactive devices.** The Furbo Dog Camera and other products allow you to see your dog, as well as vocally interact with her and use the treat-dispensing feature. Additionally, some companies claim to provide other valuable information, allowing owners to catch burglars and save their dogs from life-threatening fires and toxin ingestions.

- **Pet entertainment.** There are TV, video, radio and CD forms of entertainment for your dog to watch and/or listen to. Some dogs seem to see objects shown on a screen; others do not. Test this with your dog before you spend big money on an entertainment system.

- **Wireless doggie doorbell.** There are several of these on the market, easily found on Amazon. They allow your dog to ring a bell at the door, without expensive or complicated wiring, to get your attention when she needs to go out, even if it is to chase squirrels. The wireless bells allow your dog to signal you while you have the receiver in another room. Some, such as Pebble Smart, can dispense treats, rewarding your dog for getting your attention.

MORE BOOKS BY REVODANA PUBLISHING

Little Kids and Their Big Dogs: Volumes 1, 2 and 3

The Leonberger: A Comprehensive Guide to the Lion King of Breeds

Everyone's Guide to the Bullmastiff

The Official Book of the Neapolitan Mastiff

The Afghan Hound: Interviews with the Breed Pioneers

The Best of Babbie: The Wicked Wisdom of Babbie Tongren, the Afghan Hound's Sharpest Wit

Your Rhodesian Ridgeback Puppy: The Ultimate Guide to Finding, Rearing and Appreciating the Best Companion Dog in the World

Exploring the Tibetan Mastiff: A Love Letter in Photographs

ESPECIALLY FOR CHILDREN

Peyton Goes to the Dog Show

How the Rhodesian Ridgeback Got Its Ridge

Visit www.revodanapublishing.com